THE
MAKING OF AMERICA
SERIES

CLEVELAND HEIGHTS
THE MAKING OF AN URBAN SUBURB

CAIN PARK, 1948. An overflow crowd watched a lavish production in the outdoor amphitheater. (Cleveland Press Collection.)

ON THE COVER: *HOME OF MARCUS M. BROWN, C. 1900. The developer and his family posed in front of his home that looks much like this today. (Western Reserve Historical Society, Cleveland, Ohio.)*

To Susan,
Best wishes,
Marian J. Morton

THE
MAKING OF AMERICA
SERIES

CLEVELAND HEIGHTS

THE MAKING OF AN URBAN SUBURB

MARIAN J. MORTON

ARCADIA

Published by Arcadia Publishing,
an imprint of Tempus Publishing, Inc.
2 Cumberland Street
Charleston, SC 29401

Printed in Great Britain.

Library of Congress Catalog Card Number: 2002105518

For all general information contact Arcadia Publishing at:
Telephone 843-853-2070
Fax 843-853-0044
E-Mail sales@arcadiapublishing.com

For customer service and orders:
Toll-Free 1-888-313-2665

Visit us on the Internet at http://www.arcadiapublishing.com

CONTENTS

ACKNOWLEDGMENTS

I owe many people many thanks for help with this book.

To John Carroll University for its continued support of my research, especially the George G. Grauel Fellowship, which gave me a semester off to finish this book.

For gracious assistance with research: Dr. Judith Cetina of the Cuyahoga County Archives, James W. Garrett IV, Heights Community Congress staff.

For invaluable editorial advice and direction: Deanna Bremer, Ken Goldberg, Anne Kugler, and especially Kay Heylman for her wit, patience, and expertise.

For generous help with the photographs: Deanna Bremer, Cedar Hill Baptist Church, Claudio Caviglia (general manager, Oakwood Club), Cleveland State University Special Collections staff, Euclid Avenue Christian Church, Hugh Fisher, Forest Hill Church, Sue Hanson (director of Special Collections at Case Western Reserve University), Mimi Henry, Patricia Hoffman, Hope Lutheran Church, Mona Kolesar, Karen Laborde, Paul Lauritzen and Coventry PEACE, Jennifer Nieves (of the Dittrick Medical History Center, Case Western Reserve University), Joanne O'Brien (director of Communications and Marketing, Cleveland Heights–University Heights Board of Education), Kara Hamley O'Donnell (historic preservation planner, City of Cleveland Heights), Colleen and Dwight Olsen, Joe and Marcia Polevoi (High Tide, Rock Bottom), Pam Raack (Public Relations, City of Cleveland Heights), John Grabowski, Kermit Pike, and Anne Salcich (Western Reserve Historical Society staff), and Lynn Weygandt.

Special thanks to two extraordinary and extraordinarily generous photographers, Susie Kaeser, executive director of Reaching Heights, and Roy Woda.

Finally, this book is dedicated to the memory of my father, David L. Johnson Jr.

INTRODUCTION

On my desk sits a brilliant blue coffee mug on which are inscribed these words: "Cleveland Heights, Ohio . . . unique . . . vital . . . historic . . . neighborly . . . artistic . . . eclectic . . . progressive . . . diverse." With equal accuracy and perhaps more candor, we might add: "once elitist . . . often quarrelsome . . . sometimes divided by race or religion . . . definitely aging." This is a story of that place.

Cleveland Heights is a suburb of Cleveland, 6 miles east of its Public Square. Cleveland Heights comprises 8.1 square miles. Since 1930, its population has been over 50,000. The "heights" are the hills that slope down to the city of Cleveland and constitute the suburb's western boundary. On the south, Cleveland Heights is bounded by the Shaker Lakes and Doan Brook. To the north of Cleveland Heights lies East Cleveland; to the east, the smaller cities of South Euclid and University Heights.

Its founding fathers chose a name for Cleveland Heights that defined its suburban identity. It was, first and foremost, identified with Cleveland, then a thriving industrial metropolis and the center of the region's cultural and economic life. Second, however, the new community was on "the heights," above and apart from Cleveland's smokestacks, railroad tracks, and working-class residents. "The heights" referred both to the sloping hills and to the suburb's social and economic elevation above the urban area: "Up on the heights" meant more than a ride up the hill.

Suburbs like Cleveland Heights were born in the last decades of the nineteenth century. Millions of Americans worked in cities, but they were often unpleasant places to live, even for the very wealthy. Huge factories belched smoke into the air and pollutants into the water. Railroad tracks and commercial establishments entered even the most exclusive neighborhoods. Throngs of working people came to cities in pursuit of jobs. Often these people were European immigrants, more and more often from southern or eastern Europe with markedly foreign languages, religions, and customs. Their distinctive neighborhoods encroached into those of native-born Americans. City streets were crowded and dirty; crime and disease were frequent. Social services did not provide adequately for those in need; their poverty became visible to other urban dwellers. Improved transportation—most significantly, the electric streetcar after the 1880s—allowed people to work in the city, yet live elsewhere. And those who could afford it began the great exodus from the city to the suburbs. Although near a city, a suburb was intended to be its antithesis: no factories or commerce but homes, preferably single-family homes; no dirt and pollution but grass and trees, which represented a return to nature; no oddly dressed, oddly behaved strangers but well-to-do, well-behaved persons.

Cleveland's first suburbs developed in East Cleveland Township, where Cleveland Heights also had its beginnings. In the mid-nineteenth century, the township was a small community of farms, vineyards, and quarries. In the post–Civil War period, as Cleveland became a boisterous industrial metropolis, affluent Clevelanders moved to the township villages of Glenville, Collinwood, and Collamer\East Cleveland to live closer to nature and farther from the smoky city and its diverse residents. That same desire provided the immediate impetus for the founding in 1901 of the hamlet of Cleveland Heights on the fourth and last glacial terrace south of Lake Erie. Here in this sparsely settled, isolated countryside owned by substantial families like the Silsbys, Minors, Comptons, and Taylors, ambitious entrepreneurs and city officials envisioned a suburb for Cleveland's elite. Capitalizing on the social aspirations of their clientele, developers and real estate agents promised an exclusive and exclusively residential suburban retreat from urban problems. So promising did they make Cleveland Heights sound that many others joined the elite. Suburban newcomers of varying class, religious, ethnic, and racial backgrounds changed the suburb. So did other forces: technology, especially the streetcar and the automobile, politics, depressions, and wars. Instead of a homogeneous suburb for Anglo-Americans, Cleveland Heights quickly became a community of widely, perhaps wildly, divergent neighborhoods and people. A century after achieving its political independence, Cleveland Heights has become a place that its founders could not have imagined: an "inner-ring urban suburb" that has gracious homes of architectural distinction, attractive green parks, and distinguished public buildings but also a dwindling population of very diverse, less wealthy residents, aging housing stock, and commercial districts in need of economic revitalization.

The inscription on my coffee mug notwithstanding, the history of Cleveland Heights is not unique. Older suburbs such as Lakewood, Shaker Heights, and other members of the First Suburbs Consortium, as well as communities like Chestnut Hill in Philadelphia, Pennsylvania, and Scarsdale, New York, have experienced similar changes, beginning as elite retreats from the city and evolving into suburbs with urban characteristics. The histories of some of these communities are listed in my bibliography.

That is not to say that Cleveland Heights is not special, especially for those of us who have roots here. My grandfather and father grew up here; so did my four children; so has one of my grandsons. I have lived here myself for 37 years.

Telling this story has been full of the pleasures and pitfalls of writing about a place where I have lived long and for which I care deeply. The pleasures include the discovery of unfamiliar chapters of the past, such as the significance of the

Jewish presence and the community's heroic efforts during the Depression and World War II. The pitfalls, always present in local history, include the tendency to get nostalgic and omit the bad stuff, such as the racially inspired crimes of the 1960s. I have tried to be as objective as possible, believing that it is more useful to describe a real community than to write a fairy tale.

Other caveats to the readers include these. First, although I have relied on a wide variety of sources, I have chosen what to include and what to omit. If I have forgotten a favorite person, event, or institution, I urge readers to write about those themselves. Second, as I indicate in my acknowledgments, I have had generous help from Cleveland Heights City Hall and the Cleveland Heights–University Heights Board of Education, but this is not the authorized version of the city's past.

Living here has never been dull. I hope I haven't made it sound that way.

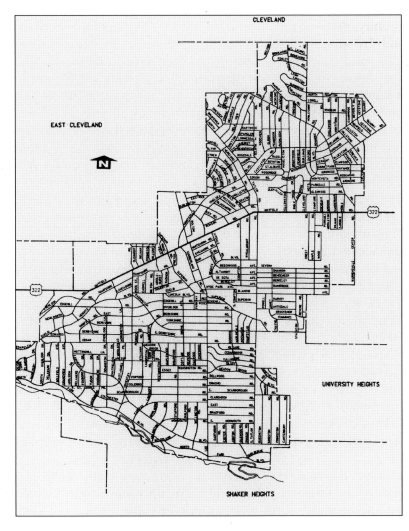

CITY OF CLEVELAND HEIGHTS, 2002. *This street map shows the current boundaries of the suburb.*

1. First Suburbs
East Cleveland Township, 1847–1901

The history of Cleveland Heights begins in East Cleveland Township, described in 1879 by historian Crisfield Johnson as "a delightful suburb of [Cleveland]."[1] The township itself was founded in 1847 after dense forests had been cleared, competing claims to the territory had been settled, and rough highways connected the township to the city. In the years following the Civil War as Cleveland became a smoky, noisy, industrial metropolis, well-to-do Clevelanders escaped the city by building summer homes, lakefront retreats, a golf club, and cemetery in the East Cleveland villages of Glenville, Collinwood, and Collamer\East Cleveland. These became Cleveland's first east-side suburbs.

East Cleveland Township lay within the Western Reserve of Connecticut, a 3,333,699-acre parcel of land that extended along the southern shores of Lake Erie, 120 miles west from the Pennsylvania line and south to Youngstown, Akron, New London, and Willard. This tract had once been the property of the colony of Connecticut, part of a grant in 1662 from the British monarch Charles II that extended across the American continent from "sea to sea."

The generous but vague grant ignored the presence of Native Americans, the country's first human inhabitants. In the early decades of the seventeenth century, the Erie Indians controlled the territory along the lake shore from Erie, Pennsylvania, to the Cuyahoga River. The lake abounded with fish; the deep forests, with deer and bears. The sandy soil closest to the lake could successfully be planted with crops; bluffs along the river could be fortified against enemies. According to Indian legend, re-told by French Jesuits, the Eries were destroyed in 1654 by the Iroquois Nations, neighbors to the west. The year before, the Eries had burned at the stake a member of the Onondaga tribe. To avenge this death, Iroquois warriors marched through the forests and sailed their canoes down the lake to the fortress within which the Eries had retreated, perhaps in the vicinity of today's Cleveland. There, armed with European weapons as well as bows and arrows and tomahawks, the Iroquois made their attack, scaled the palisade walls, entered the fort, and butchered Erie men, women, and children. Any survivors were burned alive. The Iroquois claimed the Eries' land east of the Cuyahoga,

EAST CLEVELAND TOWNSHIP, 1874. The atlas shows the boundaries of East Cleveland Township and the owners of substantial properties in what will become Cleveland Heights. (Western Reserve Historical Society, Cleveland, Ohio.)

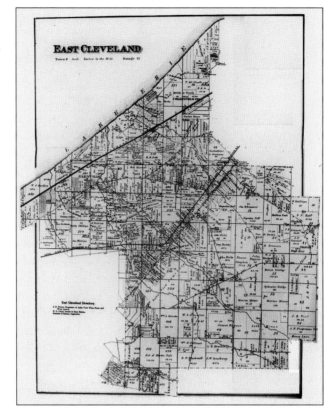

which became their hunting grounds, and then returned to their home in central New York State. The area west of the Cuyahoga was the hunting ground of the Ottawas, Chippewas, and Pottawattamies.

The first Europeans in the region were French missionaries and traders. French explorer Robert Cavelier de La Salle sailed his vessel, the *Griffin*, from Buffalo west on Lake Erie in the summer of 1678. He and some of his men disembarked to build trading posts in what became Illinois territory. The *Griffin* never returned, perhaps sunk in the treacherous lake waters, perhaps with all its crew destroyed by hostile Iroquois. La Salle returned on foot along the lake shore to the French base on the St. Lawrence River in 1679. Three years later, he returned to Illinois territory and from there, made his famous voyage of discovery down the Mississippi to the Gulf of Mexico, adding the territory of Louisiana to the French empire.

Northern Ohio became disputed territory in the series of wars between the British and the French known as the French and Indian wars. The various Indian tribes sided now with one European belligerent, now with the other. The British victory over the French in the last of these conflicts in 1763 and then over the Indian chief Pontiac in 1765 finally established this frontier area as British territory. In turn, the colonists' defeat of the British in the American Revolution in 1783 secured the Western Reserve for the United States and opened it up for settlement.

First, however, Indian claims to these western lands had to be resolved. The Iroquois relinquished their hunting grounds east of the Cuyahoga River in 1784; the Wyandots, Delawares, Chippewas, and Ottawas, their territory to the west of the river in 1785. Definitive claims to the Indian lands, however, were established only after the defeat of western tribes by General Anthony Wayne at the Battle of Fallen Timbers in 1795.

In 1786, Connecticut had ceded to the new government of the United States all of its own claims to western lands, except for the acres of the Western Reserve; these it reserved for its own use. Connecticut then sold most of these acres to the Connecticut Land Company, setting aside the proceeds for its public schools. The funds from the sale of the remaining 500,000 acres to the west of Cleveland were to be used to compensate Connecticut residents whose homes had been burned to the ground during the American Revolution; this area is still called the Firelands.

The surveyors of the Connecticut Land Company, led by Moses Cleaveland, founded what became the city of Cleveland in 1796. The site at the confluence of Lake Erie and the Cuyahoga River promised commercial success since waterways were the chief means of transporting goods and people. Around the common that

CLEVELAND'S PUBLIC SQUARE, 1896. *The triumphal arch on Public Square was built to commemorate the city's centennial when Cleveland's thriving industries made it the center of the region's economy. (Case Western Reserve University Special Collections.)*

became Public Square, the surveyors laid out the streets that became the residential and commercial center of town. The remainder of the land company's territory was divided into orderly tracts and allotments that extended several miles to the east. This vast grid of lots that grew bigger in proportion to their distance from Cleveland's center was designed for easy sale.

Cuyahoga County was formed in 1807, and East Cleveland Township, 40 years later. The township's irregular boundaries originally were Willson Avenue (East 55th) on the west, Euclid Township (approximately where the city of Euclid is today) on the east, and Newburg and Warrensville Townships on the south (approximately Euclid Avenue and Fairmount Boulevard). East Cleveland Township's most important boundary was Lake Erie on the north.

The lake determined the township's shape and to a large extent, its residents' livelihoods. The land rose gradually south from the lake on four glacial terraces. Closest to the lake, the soil was sandy; farthest away, it was heavy with clay and filled with stones. Quarrying became profitable. The lake waters moderated the temperature, staving off the brutal winter cold and the scorching summer heat endured farther inland. Vineyards flourished. Five creeks flowed north down the terraces into the lake: Doan Brook; Dugway Brook; a creek variously known as the Minor Creek\Haycox Quarry Creek, Duffy Creek, and then Eddy Road Creek; Nine Mile Creek; and farthest east, Euclid Creek. These creeks often became mill sites and centers of settlement.

Like the rest of the Western Reserve, the territory that became East Cleveland Township was only sparsely settled at the beginning of the nineteenth century. In 1804, there were only a handful of families in residence. Others soon joined them, however, and most of these first recorded white settlers were native-born immigrants from the East. Nathaniel Doan came from Connecticut and had been part of Moses Cleaveland's original surveying team. He was a blacksmith and received an allotment from the Connecticut Land Company on the condition that he continue to ply his useful trade. In 1809, Doan purchased 100 acres along Euclid Avenue at about East 105th and East 107th Streets in what is now University Circle. He moved his family there to escape the malaria-ridden center of Cleveland and opened a tavern in the small settlement that became known as Doan's Corners. His brother Timothy, a retired sea captain, arrived in 1801; he became a justice of the peace. Asa Dille and his brother David came from Pennsylvania in 1804. In that year, John Shaw and Thomas McIlrath arrived from Washington County, Pennsylvania. Shaw, born in a factory town in England, adapted quickly to farming; he also became a teacher and left to the community the land for Shaw Academy. McIlrath became an innkeeper and a shop-owner. These men had large families, and they and their sons played prominent roles in the growing settlement. They founded businesses and Protestant churches, served in the militia, and were elected to school boards and township and county governments.

East Cleveland Township was not an easy place to get to or live in. The journey by land was long and arduous; fallen timbers and deep mud made roads almost

EAST CLEVELAND HOMES, 1901. The suburban elite lived in these gracious Euclid Avenue homes. (Western Reserve Historical Society, Cleveland, Ohio.)

impassable, even for oxen. The shallow waters of Lake Erie were dangerous. Sudden winds overturned boats, and the lake's bottom is still littered with ships, their cargoes, and passengers. On land, howling wolves, prowling bears, wild panthers, stealthy rattlesnakes, and curious Indians greeted the newcomers. Until ground could be ploughed and crops harvested, men shot wild game for food. Women were sometimes left alone to fend for themselves while men sought supplies or work. The wife of Abraham Norris, awakened one night by shrill squeals, discovered a bear trying to carry away the family's pig; she frightened him off by setting a small fire. The woods of elm, maple, oak, ash, hickory, and chestnut were dense and mysterious. In pursuit of stray cattle, the wife of Timothy Eddy got lost one autumn evening; search parties were unsuccessful, but she returned unharmed in the morning, having spent the night with the wandering cows. Although pioneer women bore their hardships stoically, one woman became so homesick that she packed herself and her children into a wagon and headed back to Connecticut; when the hired driver became ill, she took the horse and travelled on alone until she reached her destination several weeks later.[2]

Settlement of this area was also briefly discouraged by the War of 1812. After the American Revolution, the British had not relinquished their claims to forts built along the western frontier. The British presence irritated Americans, who believed that the British continued to incite Indian attacks on frontier settlements such as Cleveland. Although the greater battles were fought elsewhere, the Great Lakes became the scene of conflicts between the Americans and the British stationed in Canada. East Clevelanders saw no military action, but those who lived along the lake claimed to have heard the guns of Oliver Hazard Perry's successful attack on the British fleet 75 miles away at Put-in-Bay on September 10, 1813. Andrew Jackson's victory over the British at New Orleans in 1815 symbolically ended the war, but only after the British had invaded and burned the buildings of the federal government, inspiring the hasty retreat of Congress and President James Madison. Their safety from Indians and the British finally assured, Americans continued to move west along the lake shores and inland into Cuyahoga County.

By 1850, Cleveland had become a bustling port city with a population of 17,034. Tied to cities to the east and west by the lake and to the south by the Ohio and Erie Canal, Cleveland had established itself as a significant Great Lakes commercial center. Grain, produce, livestock, lumber, and manufactured goods piled high on its wharves and in its warehouses along the Cuyahoga River. The first trains entered the city in 1851; they soon overshadowed the canal's economic importance, linking Cleveland to farther markets faster.

At mid-century, East Cleveland Township had a population of 2,313,[3] and its days as a frontier settlement were over. Comfortable frame houses had replaced most of the log cabins. Farms, vineyards, small factories, and mills dotted the countryside, which was still heavily wooded.

Churches and taverns were the community's first centers of social life. Drivers of farm wagons and stagecoach passengers stopped at local taverns, good places for folks to gather and hear the latest news. East Cleveland boasted several taverns owned by pillars of the community including Nathaniel Doan and Thomas McIlrath. The first church meetings were held at Doan's home (perhaps in the

SUBURBAN ELEGANCE, 1874. A summer home in Glenville allowed its owner to escape from the city but retain its comforts and amenities. (Cleveland State University.)

15

tavern itself). The first church structure (Congregational, then Presbyterian) was built in 1810 in the village of Collamer; Doan and his wife were founding members. This First Presbyterian Church of Collamer was noted for its strictness: "In the summer of 1811 nearly all the members publicly acknowledged their wrong-doing in permitting their children to attend the fourth of July ball."[4] The Baptists organized next, in 1820, and a year later, built a frame church at Euclid Creek; their pastor was paid in bushels of wheat and apples. The Disciples of Christ established a flourishing church in 1829 that quickly became the parent church for several others in the area.

Most township farms and businesses were located on or near the Buffalo Road, originally an Indian path, which ran parallel to the lake shore (but not so close as to get enmeshed in the swamps) from Cleveland's Public Square east through Pennsylvania to New York State. The road was laid out by the trustees of Cleveland Township in 1815 but was not passable enough to be recognized as a highway by the State of Ohio until 1832. Soon named Euclid Street, this road linked East Cleveland residents to Cleveland and other towns along the lake shore to the east. Euclid Street became the economic lifeline for East Cleveland farmers.

Township farmers raised a variety of crops. Cyrus Ford arrived in 1841 from Cummington, Massachusetts, after a failed experiment in breeding silkworms in Massillon. He bought two 100-acre farms, one on Euclid Street and one on Mayfield Road. In 1845, his son Henry described the farm to his uncle back in Massachusetts: its sandy soil was "well adapted to raising corn, rye, vines, and fruit." The other lots were suited only for raising timber. Like all farmers, the Fords were dependent on the fickle northeast Ohio weather. In 1845, a late frost and then a long drought devastated their hay, wheat, and corn; the sheep and cattle also suffered. The fruit trees, however, were hardy and reliable: "Peaches are as plenty as the stones in old Cummington. . . . Apples, peaches, pears, plums, grapes grow to greater perfection here than in any other section of my acquaintance," boasted Henry's brother, Horace.[5]

In 1852, the Cleveland, Painesville and Ashtabula Railroad connected Cleveland to Erie, Pennsylvania, passing through East Cleveland Township close to the lake shore. The railroad (later the Lake Shore and Michigan South and later still, the New York Central) strengthened the economic connections between the city and the township, making the township itself a busy shipping point and attracting new businesses and residents.

East Clevelanders also had political and cultural connections to Cleveland, whose residents enthusiastically supported the movement that sought to curtail the evils of alcohol by controlling its sale and consumption and less enthusiastically, the cause of freeing the slave. Horatio Ford, another of Cyrus's sons, attended lectures on both temperance and antislavery in Cleveland, in 1845 hearing the famous Abby Kelley, one of the few women to give public lectures in this era. Horatio himself spoke at the Cleveland Lyceum, which sponsored lectures on contemporary political and moral issues for young men. Henry Ford self-righteously described his neighbors: "East Cleveland is principally inhabited

HORATIO C. FORD'S HOME, 1874. The artist portrays a comfortable home with a barn and orchards although Euclid Avenue was not isolated or rural by this time. (Cleveland State University.)

by drunkards, infidels, and locos, with all of whom we have no fellowship, being on the contrary staunch supporters of religion and . . . abolitionists. . . . But we hope, with the aid of a few citizens . . . to change the morals . . . and reputation of our new neighborhood."[6]

Despite this ungenerous assessment, East Cleveland township did have its own cultural life. Horatio Ford attended choir concerts, meetings of the East Cleveland Antislavery Society, and all-day Sunday worship services at the Euclid Avenue Congregational Church, where he also taught Sunday school. Both Henry and Horatio Ford taught school during the winter months when they and their students could be spared from their farming chores. In 1859, the township school district enrolled 1,269 students in its ten school buildings, two of them shared with Euclid Township. The average daily attendance, however, was less than half of that. Horatio often complained that even during the short school year, his students' attendance was irregular. On December 29, 1845, he grumbled: "Found my school turned ends up by the holidays [the students] have enjoyed. I feel like leaving one more good wish for those careful parents or wise children, whose care or wisdom presents such an everlasting irregularity of attendance. I wish the former would send or keep at home, the latter come or stay at home, and make a business of it."[7]

During these decades, East Cleveland's elected trustees, treasurers, and assessors tended to be native-born men of substance, if not great wealth. The same families—Ford, McIlrath, and Doan, for instance—often held elected office. In 1850, all officials described themselves to the census-taker as farmers, except the grocer Daniel R. Hildreth. In 1860, Darius Adams, the wealthiest of the officials, listed his occupation as carpenter and valued his real estate and personal property at $10,600. In 1870, trustees had a wider range of occupations, as did residents as a whole. The wealthiest trustee was Nathan Post, a "butcher," worth $15,000; M.A. Bard, an "ice dealer," valued his assets at $4,000. Although the federal census noted 1,366 foreign-born and 68 "colored" among East Cleveland's population of 5,050, their names do not appear on the lists of office-holders.[8]

When President Abraham Lincoln asked for volunteers for the Union Army in April 1861 after the fall of Fort Sumter, East Cleveland Township men were among the 10,000 from Cuyahoga County who signed up. Sons of the founding families—Fords, Shaws, Cozads, and McIlraths—served in the 103rd, the 124th, the 128th, the 150th, and the 177th Infantry, the Sixth Cavalry, and the First Ohio Volunteer Light Artillery. Township women doubtless joined the Soldiers Aid Society of Northern Ohio, which raised funds for medical and other supplies for soldiers and their families. As in the War of 1812, the battles were fought elsewhere. But Cleveland was the site of seven Civil War camps. Camp Cuyahoga, where the militia drilled and trained, was at Willson's Grove on the western border of East Cleveland Township. When news of the Confederate army's surrender reached Cleveland on the morning of April 10, 1865, residents celebrated on Public Square, raising the Union flag over Old Stone Church. April 14 was declared a day of thanksgiving, observed with church services and public speeches. On April 28, the funeral train carrying the body of the assassinated Lincoln home to Springfield, Illinois, passed through the city.

The war transformed Cleveland. The demand for war materials hastened the city's industrialization. Flourishing oil refineries, iron and steel foundries, and chemical plants attracted immigrants from Ireland and Germany and newcomers from nearby country towns, crowding neighborhoods and straining private and public charities. Railroads criss-crossed the city. Lake fleets steamed in and out of Cleveland ports. Cleveland's population more than doubled from 1860 (43,417) to 1870 (92,829). Some of that increase came from Cleveland's annexation of parts of Brooklyn and Newburgh Townships. (Cleveland had annexed Ohio City in 1854.) Annexation was commonly used by nineteenth-century cities to expand their boundaries; residents of annexed communities voted for annexation to gain services such as city water and police and fire protection.

In this post-war period, Cleveland sought to expand its boundaries to the east. About 4 miles east of Public Square on Euclid in East Cleveland Township lay the commercial and residential center of Doan's Corners. The community included homes on large lots with pastures, orchards, and stables that fronted on Euclid and the north-south side streets; two general stores, one of which housed the post office; three churches (Methodist, Disciples of Christ, and Congregational); a cemetery; the still-bustling tavern once run by Nathaniel Doan; a blacksmith shop; and the Doan Street School, where Henry Ford taught. To the east along Euclid were larger lots, the sites of the orchards and gardens of the Fords and the Cozads. Stone from the quarries to the east was sold at the Corners. Members of

the Shaker Community in Warrensville Township traded there. Early industries—
a clock factory, gristmill, and tannery—were replaced in the 1860s by small iron
foundries. The woods, wild life, and ponds gave Doan's Corners a rural quality,
but by the 1860s, the homes of its most substantial citizens were built in the latest
urban styles with landscaped grounds. In 1866, Doan's Corners became part of
the newly incorporated Village of East Cleveland. In 1872, this new village was
absorbed into the city of Cleveland when it annexed a large section of East
Cleveland Township west of Willson.

Still distant from Cleveland's smokestacks and factories, the remainder of East
Cleveland Township became defined as suburban. The township villages were the
logical next stop for affluent Clevelanders, who escaped the city by moving east
on Euclid Street, which was renamed Euclid Avenue in 1865. Within the city
limits, the avenue was known as Millionaires' Row, the address of the men who
had profited from Cleveland's booming economy. Here lived the city's wealthiest
merchants, industrialists, and professionals: entrepreneur John D. Rockefeller;
members of the Louis H. and Solon Severance families; banker Daniel P. Eells;
inventor and philanthropist Jeptha Homer Wade; and a host of others who left
their names and some of their fortunes to Cleveland's cultural and charitable
institutions. On the Avenue these men and their families built elaborate mansions
and vast Protestant cathedrals, raced their carriages, socialized, inter-married, and
solidified family and financial connections. Euclid Avenue's front yards were
defined by iron fences; on the avenue's north side, backyards stretched to Lake
Erie. The avenue's glory days lasted from 1850 to 1910, but they determined the
migration pattern of Cleveland's elite for much longer.

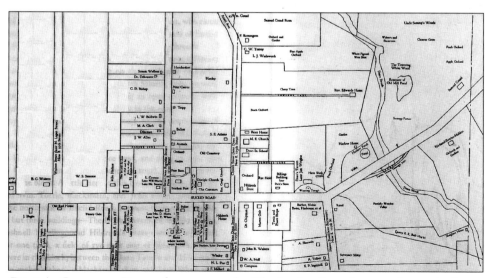

*DOAN'S CORNERS. Drawn from memory by Charles Asa Post, the map pictures the farms,
churches, and stores of this small community in 1857 in what is now University Circle.
(Cleveland State University.)*

19

EAST CLEVELAND RAILWAY HORSE CAR, 1874. Horse cars linked downtown Cleveland to East Cleveland Township. (Cleveland State University.)

Changes in transportation also facilitated an eastward suburban migration. Passengers could already travel from Public Square to East Cleveland Township by stagecoach or railroad, and beginning in 1860, they could take an East Cleveland Railway Company horse car out Euclid, bypassing from 1862 to 1884 the avenue's most fashionable section. When the cars electrified during the late 1880s, the commute became even quicker, although it was still too costly for most people.

Although East Cleveland Township remained primarily agricultural, some enterprising residents had begun to see that farmland could become profitable residential development. According to an 1872 East Cleveland school census, most of the students' parents were farmers (101), laborers (118), gardeners (59), and stone cutters (12), reminders of the original economy of the country village. Indicative of economic change were the 82 carpenters and 37 "manufacturers," owners of mills and small factories, and 99 merchants, who bought and sold the products of these farms and factories. Professional men also sent their children to East Cleveland schools: 13 lawyers, 7 doctors, 5 clergymen, and 2 teachers. Thirty-seven men described themselves as "agents, insurance, Real Estate, etc.," three as "land holders," and a dozen as "capitalists."[9] These men became the first suburban developers.

An early harbinger of the township's suburbanization was the establishment in 1869 of Lake View Cemetery on 200 acres east of Doan's Corners and south of Euclid Avenue. The tract was purchased by a group headed by Jeptha Homer Wade, who later donated 63 acres to the City of Cleveland for the park named after him. Located high on a bluff, the cemetery offered a fine view of Lake Erie and the settled areas to its east and west. Like other urban parks and the suburbs of the near future, the garden cemetery was designed as an escape from the city. Its rolling hills, manicured grass, curving roadways, grand Victorian structures, and classical statuary provided models for the suburban landscape to come. Lots sold slowly at first partly because Lake View was so far away (6 miles from Public Square) and partly because it had an elitist reputation. The cemetery became more accessible when the electric streetcar reached its Euclid Avenue gates, and more popular after it became home to the assassinated President James A. Garfield and his family. Lake View's signature sculpture, the massive Garfield Monument, was dedicated in 1890.

John D. Rockefeller also saw the profitable possibilities of real estate in the township. In 1872, at the beginning of his career at Standard Oil of Ohio, Rockefeller bought a water cure hotel high on a bluff to the east of Doan's Corners and south of Euclid. He also built a luxury commuter rail line, the Lakeview and Collamer Railroad, to transport clientele to the hotel. Although the railroad made the trip easier, the hotel never made money. (Perhaps the sight of Lake View Cemetery to the west was a disincentive.) Undaunted, Rockefeller turned the hotel into his family's summer home and estate, named it Forest Hill, and built winding pathways, ponds, and a golf course on his vast property. He eventually bought more than 700 acres in East Cleveland Township for

JOHN D. ROCKEFELLER.
Rockefeller and his family were
early suburban developers.
(Cleveland State University.)

GLENVILLE, 1874. Urban dwellers were drawn to the lake and trees of suburban Glenville. (Cleveland State University.)

investment purposes. Rockefeller and his son John D. Rockefeller Jr. would play crucial roles in the development of Cleveland Heights.

In the 1870s, the country villages of Glenville, Collinwood, and Collamer became suburban retreats for the wealthy. The village of Glenville, north of Doan's Corners at about St. Clair and East 105th, incorporated in 1872. Originally a center for trading farm produce, Glenville in 1870 became the site of a famous harness racing track and the Northern Ohio Fairgrounds, where local farmers annually showed off their produce and livestock. These attractions, and Glenville's proximity to the lake, induced affluent Clevelanders to build summer homes there. D.J. Lake's *Atlas of Cuyahoga County*, published in 1874, captured the transformation of Glenville into a "romantic" suburb—"romantic" in the nineteenth-century sense of an escape into an idealized natural landscape. Two handsome "summer residences" in Glenville faced Lake Erie. The home of Mrs. H.F. Clark was an elaborate Italianate with an imposing cupola, formal landscaping, and large outbuildings; George A. Benedict's home was simpler but had an inviting front veranda. By the 1890s, the streetcar provided an easy commute downtown. In 1895, Glenville gained additional luster among Cleveland's elite when the Cleveland Golf Club opened there.

To the east along the Lake Shore railroad line, the village of Collinwood grew up around the Lake Shore's repair shops and roundhouses. By the end of the 1870s, this settlement of 1,500 persons had its own post office as well as three public schools, churches, several shops, meat markets, groceries, livery stables, harness shops, drugstores, and a hotel.

To the south of Glenville and Collinwood and linked to the southern section of East Cleveland Township by Noble and Taylor Roads, the village of Collamer also became a densely settled neighborhood. In 1860, the village boasted a host of social and cultural institutions in addition to stores, taverns, and mills. So many Protestant churches (Presbyterian, Episcopalian, Disciples of Christ, and Congregational) located there that the village became known as "Saint's Row." The 151 pupils of Collamer's Union School made it the township's largest. The village was also the site of Shaw Academy; this high school began as a private academy and joined the East Cleveland public school system in 1877. Collamer claimed about a thousand residents in 1879 and retained its rural character despite its shops and mills. Consequently, the village became "a special favorite of Clevelanders desirous of a more retired life than that of the city. The main road [Euclid Avenue] . . . to [Cleveland] is thickly studded with pleasant farm houses, and with handsome residences situated on small but most desirable tracts," declared Crisfield Johnson.[10]

Clevelanders, especially those who could afford it, might have had good reason to desire a "more retired" life. In 1890, Cleveland was the tenth largest city in the country. Of its population of 261,353, only one-fourth were native born of native parentage; 97,095 had been born in other countries. Germans still constituted the largest group of newcomers. Fewer came from Great Britain and Ireland than in earlier decades; more, from southeastern Europe. The city's black population

EAST CLEVELAND PRESBYTERIAN CHURCH, 1901. East Cleveland boasted several handsome churches like this one. This church remains at this site. (Western Reserve Historical Society, Cleveland, Ohio.)

ROCKEFELLER SUMMER HOME. From the many porches of this spacious structure there was a splendid view of Lake Erie, just to the north. This became Rockefeller's summer home when it failed as a water cure hotel. (Cleveland State University.)

reached 3,035.[11] Huge factories clustered along railroad tracks and the winding Cuyahoga River, polluting the air with smoke and the water with industrial waste. Electric streetcars that ran east and west and north and south hastened the out-migration of those who could afford the fare.

But new downtown buildings, including the elegant glass-enclosed Euclid Avenue Arcade, the imposing Soldiers' and Sailors' Monument on Public Square, and two massive armories, signalled that Cleveland had grand aspirations. Those aspirations were further expressed in the city's continuing efforts to annex adjoining territories. In 1892, Cleveland encroached further into East Cleveland Township, annexing a tract bounded roughly by University Circle, Lakeview, Cedar, and Superior Avenues. This tract included Little Italy, a colony of Italian stone-cutters immediately to the west of Lake View Cemetery.

To escape being swallowed up by the metropolis, the hamlet of Collamer incorporated as the (second) Village of East Cleveland in 1895. The village proudly retained its Euclid Avenue panache: "the village is practically an improved extension . . . of the famous Euclid Avenue," boasted the village's 1901 annual report.[12] The report also presented evidence of the eastward migration of the elite: the imposing Euclid Avenue homes, and the summer residence of Rockefeller himself, the erstwhile water cure hotel with three levels of porches to catch the lake breezes. Four East Cleveland congregations—Episcopalian, Congregational, and two Presbyterian —built imposing new places of worship; new Methodist and Baptist congregations joined them.

The village's first elected officials were ardent proponents of suburban development, recognizing that "the constant expansion of the City of Cleveland demanded more and more suburban homes." Officials paved roads, laid sidewalks, contracted with the streetcar company to extend its lines farther east, and provided gas, water, electricity, and sewers. There was no public space, however, and Lake View Cemetery was the closest thing to a village park. The village claimed 3,000 residents in 1901. In his annual message, Mayor Charles E.

Bolton urged his constituents to resist annexation by Cleveland. Vigorously differentiating his suburb from the city, Bolton pointed out that East Cleveland had "little or no politics, no saloons, no policemen, no crimes, and little of poverty. Annexation would mean saloons, crime, and increased taxation, and few if any advantages. . . . East Cleveland is a quiet retreat from the . . . busy city. . . . Here families escape from the noise, dust, smoke, and subtle poisons that always taint the air of a crowded manufacturing city." Bolton let his wife, Sarah, a poet and biographer, describe the new villages: "Tree-covered hills, crossed by a deep ravine \ Yonder a lake of blue, shaded to crimson hue \ When rays of sunset bridge the vale between. . . . Ah! Life is sweet with nature face to face."[13] With such attractions, the new suburban community grew rapidly. A decade later, East Cleveland had 10,000 residents.

By the time East Cleveland Township was founded, its residents had survived frontier hardships and political perils and formed pleasant communities that then survived the Civil War. In the post-war period, these country villages defined suburban life for later generations of Clevelanders: an escape from the city to a natural landscape, an escape that was available primarily to those that could afford homes, churches, golf clubs, and burial sites in these first suburbs. A suburban address in Glenville, Collinwood, or Collamer\East Cleveland Village represented affluence and social status.

Glenville and Collinwood, like Doan's Corners before them, were annexed by the City of Cleveland in 1905 and 1910, respectively. East Cleveland was the first of two villages in East Cleveland township to declare suburban independence. The second was Cleveland Heights.

EUCLID AVENUE IN EAST CLEVELAND VILLAGE, 1901. The suburban community was an extension east of Euclid Avenue, the famous "Millionaire's Row." (Western Reserve Historical Society, Cleveland, Ohio.)

2. THE SUBURBAN VISION
DEVELOPING CLEVELAND HEIGHTS, 1890–1921

Early developers of Cleveland Heights shared East Cleveland mayor Charles E. Bolton's compelling vision of a suburb: a place where the elite could live near the city but distant from its industry and commerce, close to nature and persons like themselves. Entrepreneur Patrick Calhoun described the golf club he established for his wealthy clientele: "[U]pon the crest of a lofty height . . . away from the noise and dirt of the city and yet within a few minutes of its heart." And developer B.R. Deming, no less eloquently, described his own allotment named after Calhoun's club: "a land of great natural beauty with well-kept lawns, tastefully treated homes . . . where more and more Clevelanders of culture and refinement want to make their homes."[1] This vision inspired the founding of Cleveland Heights in 1901 and two decades later, the suburb's first zoning legislation. For this vision, and the streetcar, had attracted to the suburb not only persons of "culture and refinement," but many others as well.

In the mid-nineteenth century, like the rest of East Cleveland Township, the area that became Cleveland Heights was farmland, quarries, and vineyards, owned by men of northern and western European descent who had come from New England, Ohio, and neighboring states and had accumulated substantial property. In the 1860 census, Sylvester Silsby, born in New Hampshire, listed his occupation as "stonecutter" and valued his property at $15,000; George Compton, a farmer and Ohio native, valued his acreage at $10,000. Ten years later, Frederick Silsby, also a farmer, had settled near his brother. Other new neighbors included Marion and Seth Minor, who together owned real estate worth $50,000. Property translated into political responsibility. The men of the Silsby and Minor households served as trustees of East Cleveland Township in the 1860s and 1870s. Charles Compton served on the East Cleveland School Board; his children attended the State Road School with the Minor and Silsby children.[2]

Lake breezes encouraged flourishing orchards and vineyards on these hillsides. Polly Taylor described the farm purchased by her family in 1850: "there are 50 acres of good timber. We have peach, plum, and nectarine trees and a large apple orchard." In 1864, John Peter Preyer bought 75 acres of farmland, moved his family into a spacious home built in the 1820s of local sandstone, and planted the vineyards for his Lake View Wine Farm. His neighbor to the south, James Haycox, operated a dairy and quarry on his 182-acre property. D.J. Lake's 1874 *Atlas of Cuyahoga County* pictured Haycox's comfortable home with a view of the lake, surrounded by mature trees and well-tended outbuildings. Seth Minor's daughter many years later remembered the family barn built in 1870, "said to be as fine as any in the state," the orchard of 240 apple trees of 40 varieties, and the "pretty picture of the cows coming up the paths."[3]

This southern part of East Cleveland Township developed more slowly than the section closer to the lake. Two decades after Collamer, Glenville, and Collinwood became suburban villages, this sparsely settled area remained rural. Its perch on the last glacial terrace gave residents a splendid view of the lake but distanced them from the villages and the railroad on the north. Steep hills kept residents economically and socially isolated from Cleveland to the west. A small railroad to haul bluestone and timber down Cedar Glen (Cedar Road hill) had failed in 1849. There was no direct stagecoach or horse car connection to downtown Cleveland. The chief thoroughfare, State (Mayfield) Road, laid out in 1828, turned east from Euclid Avenue at Doan's Corners, to Lake View Cemetery and then to the distant village of Gates Mills. Mayfield remained the suburb's central thoroughfare, but it never acted as an extension of an elite residential boulevard as Euclid Avenue did in East Cleveland.

PREYER HOUSE. *John Peter Preyer purchased this home in 1864; built c. 1825 and recently restored, it is the oldest structure in Cleveland Heights. (Cleveland Press Collection.)*

FARM OF JAMES HAYCOX, 1874. This home and outbuildings were on what is now Lee Road, just south of Superior; the quarry was on the site of Cain Park. (Cleveland State University.)

No significant commercial or residential centers developed here during the 1870s and 1880s. The only church, Fairmount Methodist established in 1875, met first in the Superior School, then in a small frame building next door. In 1904, the congregation built a simple Gothic revival structure at Hampshire and Superior Roads and became the Cleveland Heights Methodist Episcopal Church.

Two local businessmen, William L. Rice and John Hartness Brown, may have been the first to see Cleveland Heights's possibilities as an elite suburb, but the first to pursue those possibilities was Patrick Calhoun. The grandson of Vice-President John C. Calhoun of South Carolina, Calhoun was 6 feet tall with a commanding presence that inspired his contemporaries. Calhoun was the legal counsel for several railroads, and he came to Cleveland in 1890 on railroad business. According to legend, the sight of the Garfield Monument in Lake View Cemetery inspired him to plan nearby a suburban version of Millionaires' Row. He unashamedly borrowed its name and called his main thoroughfare "Euclid Boulevard" (later Euclid Heights Boulevard) and his allotment "Euclid Heights," for it would be high on a bluff overlooking the city and the lake. He quickly began to assemble the parcels for his development, which ultimately was bounded by Cedar Road on the south, Coventry on the east, Mayfield on the north, and the Cleveland city limits on the west. His largest purchase was the farm and timbering operation of Doan's Corner resident Worthy S. Streator. Calhoun also bought up properties at the top of Cedar Glen on which small developers in the 1870s had laid out, but not yet built, two modest residential neighborhoods. Neighbor and fellow real estate speculator John D. Rockefeller allegedly lent Calhoun money for the Euclid Heights development. Calhoun's models may have been the similar elite suburbs that were developed in this period along Philadelphia's Main Line and Chicago's North Shore. Closer to home, wealthy Clevelanders were building grand homes in Lakewood's Clifton Park and on the Lake Erie shore.

But a serious depression in 1893 slowed Calhoun's sales, and to make matters worse, his allotment could be most directly approached from Cleveland only by narrow, muddy roads that climbed the steep hills. Calhoun knew that electric streetcars were needed to make his investment profitable. In 1890, the electric street railway had made its initial foray into the southern section of East Cleveland Township, running up Mayfield to the gates of Lake View Cemetery. But this route through Little Italy did not seem appropriate for the elegant neighborhood Calhoun planned. In 1896, therefore, Calhoun donated to the City of Cleveland property on Cedar Glen and along Euclid Avenue that linked Cleveland's emerging park system from Doan Creek and the Shaker Lakes on the east through Rockefeller Park to Gordon Park on Lake Erie. The gift also created an impressive entrance up Cedar Glen to the Euclid Heights allotment. In 1897, Calhoun built an electric street railway line up Cedar Glen and east on Euclid Heights Boulevard. Calhoun also paid for gas and water lines to be extended into his

GARFIELD MONUMENT AT LAKE VIEW CEMETERY. *The monument to the assassinated President James A. Garfield supposedly inspired Patrick Calhoun to plan his suburban development nearby. (Cleveland State University.)*

subdivision and reportedly subsidized his wealthy clients' home purchases. By 1898, some 30 lawyers, industrialists, and bankers, including some of Calhoun's investors, had built urban mansions that emulated those on Euclid Avenue. From these generous lots on "The Overlook," homeowners could see the lake, the city, and the new buildings of Case Institute of Technology and Western Reserve University down Cedar Glen in University Circle.

Calhoun took steps to ensure his development's elegance and exclusivity. Deed restrictions stipulated the cost of the home and the size of its lot and prohibited any commercial uses in the allotment. He planted thousands of trees to replace those cut down by Streator and donated the land for a small Episcopalian church, St. Alban, at Euclid Heights Boulevard and Edgehill Road. He also built the imposing Tudor-style Euclid Club in 1901 as an added amenity for Euclid Heights residents. A decade later, landscape designer E.W. Bowditch had laid out a neighborhood of gracious homes of English-influenced design on curving streets with English names—Berkshire, Derbyshire, Kenilworth, Norfolk, and Surrey.

Calhoun could not ensure the safety of these exclusive streets, however, and in 1910, Euclid Heights became the scene of a still-unsolved murder mystery involving the two men sometimes credited with being Calhoun's inspiration, Rice and Brown. Both were residents and significant investors in the allotment; Rice was also briefly a village trustee. Walking home from golf and dinner at the Euclid Club to his vast Overlook mansion on the evening of August 4, Rice was beaten, stabbed, shot, and left dying at the corner of Euclid Heights Boulevard and

EUCLID CLUB, 1911. The gracious clubhouse and golf course were intended to attract residents to the Euclid Heights allotment. (Western Reserve Historical Society, Cleveland, Ohio.)

JOHN HARTNESS BROWN HOUSE, 1917. Designed in 1896 by Alfred Hoyt Granger for the Euclid Heights investor, this is one of the few private homes left on "The Overlook." (Case Western Reserve University Special Collections.)

Derbyshire Road. Although there were many Cleveland Heights residents out and about that summer evening and neighbors thought they heard shots, no one could provide village police, unused to homicides, with useful clues. Men from Little Italy down the hill and black servants of the golf club were immediately rounded up and questioned. But others suspected the murder had been committed by someone well known to Rice, his nearest neighbor and business adversary, Brown. Not only had Rice allegedly swindled Brown out of a downtown building, but Brown arrived on the streetcar at the crime scene almost simultaneously with the police, a very suspicious coincidence. Soon after Rice's murder, Brown's own investment in the allotment went sour, and he left for England. Brown's home still stands at Edgehill and Overlook Roads. Its massive stone exterior and Gothic windows, reminiscent of the nearby Garfield Monument, are testimony to the darker sides of this elegant neighborhood: the deep-seated suspicions of strangers, especially the Italian neighbors, and the (perhaps) murderous impulses of the very wealthy.[4]

In contrast, many years later, residents recalled happy childhoods in Euclid Heights. In 1914, Dr. George Crile, founder of the Cleveland Clinic, bought Calhoun's house on Derbyshire Road. His son, Dr. George Crile Jr., an internationally known surgeon and author, recalled this enormous mansion: "a huge three-story brick palazzo, with about six servants' bedrooms, and on the second story there were seven bedrooms for the family . . . Then there were about six more bedrooms on the top floor—a ballroom, of course—and a huge living room, a big library, dining room, and then elaborate maids' quarters and butlers' quarters in the basement . . . We had two gardeners." The neighborhood was still rural. The children trapped groundhogs and rabbits, ran wild through the woods and ravines, and fished in the little brooks. After his family sold the home, Crile moved to nearby Kent Road. His neighbor Betty Moore remembered the "rowdy gang" of her childhood friends who played games in the streets and swam in the pool at the large estate of Dr. Charles Briggs, which was "very elegant with marble walls and marble fixtures and a fountain playing, bronze statues and wisteria vines."[5]

Not all residents of this new community lived in Calhoun's Euclid Heights. Less famous local entrepreneurs with more modest middle-class markets in mind also ventured early into real estate on these suburban heights. Simultaneously with Calhoun, William and Edmund Walton Jr. laid out their Cedar Heights allotment in a cow pasture off Cedar Road, just east of Cedar Glen. Its two streets, Bellfield and Grandview Avenues, were similar to the Waltons' development in Little Italy. Although the lots were small, these single and double homes were comfortable foursquares with gracious porches and interesting gables and dormers. In 1890, longtime resident James Haycox and his business partner Charles Asa Post bought a large farm at Lee and Mayfield, and successfully lobbied for the extension of the streetcar east on Mayfield from Lake View Cemetery to serve their new subdivision. Haycox and Post named their streets after the trees they had found on the old farm: Oak, Sycamore, and Whitethorn Roads.

In 1898, Marcus M. Brown, a developer from Chicago, purchased the Preyer property west of Superior for his Mayfield Heights allotment, close to both the Euclid Heights and the Mayfield streetcars. His advertisements made the same claims that Calhoun and Deming did although without their aristocratic pretensions. "Mayfield Heights [has] all city improvements, good car service, beautiful boulevarded roads, proper and adequate restrictions, pure air and the freedom of the country . . . REAL HOMES FOR REAL PEOPLE."[6] The first homes in Mayfield Heights, including Brown's own, were larger and more imposing than those built by the Waltons or Haycox and Post, but much less formal than the urban mansions of "The Overlook." Large porches and windows welcomed the suburban trees and green spaces. Brown wrote an admiring biography of John D. Rockefeller, entitled *A Study of John D. Rockefeller, The Wealthiest Man in the World . . . With His Name Left Out, the history of Education and Religion could not be written*." Brown pursued his idol into suburban real estate, although with much less success and persistence; he stayed in Cleveland Heights only a decade.

The Mayfield streetcar line encouraged other residential and commercial development along its path. At Mayfield and Superior, a small town center developed by the 1890s that became the first community gathering place. Homes clustered around a cider mill, general store, blacksmith shop, and a post office

GRANDVIEW AVENUE, c. 1893. This comfortable home sat almost alone in the rural Cedar Heights development of Grandview and Bellfield; much altered, this house still stands. (Cleveland Heights Planning Department.)

named Fairmount. O.A. Dean's home and dairy lay just west of the center. Even farther west along Mayfield at Taylor Road, members of the Severance family—Julia Severance Millikin and her husband Dr. Benjamin Millikin, and her cousin Elizabeth Severance Allen, wife of Dr. Dudley Allen—bought farms for summer homes, maintaining their year-round residences on Euclid Avenue. Louis Henry Severance, father of Elizabeth and business associate of Rockefeller, in the 1890s purchased several properties near Mayfield and Taylor; these later included the Silsby family farm at the southeast corner of the intersection.

At the beginning of the twentieth century, this area was ripe for political autonomy and further development. The residents of Euclid Heights, the most densely settled and wealthiest neighborhood in the hamlet, were probably the primary movers behind a drive for political independence from East Cleveland Township. They had reason to fear that their new neighborhood would be annexed either by the City of Cleveland or by the new Village of East Cleveland. Cleveland's 1892 annexation had brought the city into Little Italy and right to the edge of Lake View Cemetery, too close for comfort for those aspiring to build an elite suburb. In August 1900, the trustees of the township (which no longer included Glenville, Collinwood, or the Village of East Cleveland) declared that qualified residents could vote to incorporate the hamlet of Cleveland Heights. The hamlet would include the Euclid Heights allotment and much of what was left of East Cleveland Township, including the southernmost portions of Lake View Cemetery and the Rockefeller estate. On September 8, 92 men voted for hamlet status, only 4 against it.

In 1901, the citizens of Cleveland Heights (population 1,564) elected the hamlet's first trustees from among its well-to-do residents. Among them were financier J.G.W. Cowles, a resident of Calhoun's development and president of Cleveland Trust bank, Calhoun's principal lender; J.M. Spence, a large property owner and a paving and sewer contractor; William G. Phare, a real estate lawyer, banker, and owner of the general store; and longtime residents and property owners including members of the Preyer and Minor families as well as William T. Quilliams and Charles E. Gooding. Quilliams and Gooding, as trustees of East Cleveland Township, had supported the vote to allow the separate incorporation of Cleveland Heights. The hamlet became a village in 1903, and in 1909, Cleveland Heights built its first city hall, a simple but dignified brick structure on Mayfield, close to the voting booth at Mayfield and Superior where the trustees had met since 1901.

These men wished the suburb to be exclusive; their first official act in 1901 was to ban saloons that might attract a working-class clientele. But they were also investors in real estate, who had much to gain from Cleveland Heights's further

J.G.W. COWLES, 1896. Investor in and resident of Euclid Heights, Cowles was an early trustee of the hamlet of Cleveland Heights, a financial adviser to John D. Rockefeller, and president of the Cleveland Chamber of Commerce. (Case Western Reserve University Special Collections.)

AMBLER PARKWAY, 1896. These men built an impressive entrance to Ambler Heights. (Cleveland State University.)

development. Their first concerns were providing new suburbanites with urban comforts: water, sewage, streetlights, phone service, electricity, and passable roads. Most significantly, the trustees provided streetcar lines, and in the next two decades, Cleveland Heights developed as a "streetcar suburb." Streetcars made suburban living an attractive possibility for those who could afford the commute and a suburban home.

The first two streetcar franchises granted were in the suburb's elite neighborhoods, which village trustees were especially interested in promoting. In 1904, the first franchise went to the Cleveland Railway Company to extend its line farther into Calhoun's allotment: up Cedar Glen, east on Euclid Heights Boulevard to Coventry Road.

This Euclid Heights streetcar also served Ambler Heights, south across Cedar Glen from Calhoun's allotment. Its curved streets (Chestnut Hills, Elandon, Denton, Harcourt, and Devonshire Drives) were intended for well-to-do families. Like their neighbors on "The Overlook," they admired the view of the city down the hill and immediately to the west. The neighborhood, which is now called Chestnut Hills, was originally named for its first developer, Dr. Nathan Hardy Ambler, whose home was across Doan Brook on the current site of the Baldwin Filtration Plant.

In 1906, trustees granted the second streetcar franchise to the Cleveland Railway Company to extend its lines east on what is now Fairmount Boulevard through the golf course of the Euclid Club, owned by John D. Rockefeller. The streetcar's destination was the new subdivision of developers Mantis J. and Oris

P. Van Sweringen. Their tract had originally been part of "the Valley of God's Pleasure," the community of the North Union Shakers founded in 1822. When the group disbanded in 1889, their property was sold first to a group of Clevelanders, who gave it the name Shaker Heights, and then to a real estate syndicate from Buffalo, also known as the Shaker Heights Land Company. In 1905, the Van Sweringens, who had begun their real estate careers selling middle-income housing in Lakewood, began to buy and sell more expensive lots for the Shaker Heights Land Company. The brothers also planned to build and sell homes for the affluent along Fairmount Boulevard and on north-south side streets between Coventry and Lee, and in 1906, the Van Sweringens and their investors bought the entire 1,200 acres of the former Shaker community. The Shaker mills and other buildings, fallen into disrepair, were torn down, but the two manmade lakes were maintained.

In 1907, Cleveland Heights annexed the portion of the Van Sweringen development known as Shaker Village. Four years later, when the village of Shaker Heights became independent, it relinquished some of this territory to Cleveland Heights. The boundary between Shaker Heights and Cleveland Heights then ran through the middle of the Shaker Lakes. The Van Sweringen development along Fairmount, which included Fairfax, Arlington, Wellington, Stratford, and Guilford, remained in Cleveland Heights. The brothers' formula for success

FAIRMOUNT BOULEVARD, 1913. The streetcar tracks ran through this property soon to be developed as the Euclid Golf Allotment. Roxboro School appears in the distance. (Deanna Bremer and Hugh Fisher.)

SHAKER LAKE, 1896. The Van Sweringen brothers planned their exclusive development around the picturesque lakes built by the Shaker Community. (Cleveland State University.)

initiated in Cleveland Heights—careful planning, tight restrictions, high architectural standards, and reliance on public transit—would be perfected in Shaker Heights, which remained the symbol of elite suburbia long after the Van Sweringens' real estate and railroad empire collapsed during the Great Depression.

Another beneficiary of the Fairmount Boulevard streetcar was local developer B.R. Deming. In 1913, Deming presented to the village council his plans for the Euclid Golf Allotment. This was to be built to the west of the Van Sweringens' development along Fairmount Boulevard between Coventry and Cedar on the site of the former golf course, which Deming had purchased from Rockefeller. Deming's promotional materials promised exclusivity and featured photographs of large, gracious homes, insulated from each other by wide yards and mature trees. Like the Van Sweringens, Deming imposed strict guidelines. Versatile local architects Howell and Thomas designed many of these homes in a wide variety of styles, but all building plans had to be approved by Deming to insure that proportions, colors, and designs "harmonize[d] with the character of the street." These restrictions were intended to "keep the character of the neighborhood up to the highest point."[7]

Although built for a wealthy clientele, these newer homes in the southern section of the suburb were not—with some notable exceptions—the vast mansions on huge lots of "The Overlook." Calhoun had experienced financial difficulties re-creating a nineteenth-century urban boulevard in this suburban setting, and the worst of his difficulties would soon befall him. Most of the residences built in Ambler Heights and the Van Sweringen and Deming

EUCLID GOLF HOME. Howell and Thomas, the versatile architects for this Tudor Drive home, designed many residences in this allotment. (Case Western Reserve University Special Collections.)

allotments would be in American colonial revival styles (that is, pre-American Revolution English styles) that rejected the elaborate Victorian homes of the turn of the century in favor of a simpler, more modern, indigenous architecture. These gracious homes, along with the English street names, identified the suburb and its residents as affluent and Anglo-American and became the models for hundreds of later builders of much less expensive homes.

Village trustees further encouraged the development of this southern section by annexing portions of Idlewood Village in 1914 and 1915. Idlewood, Shaker, East Fairfax, Bradford, Kingston, Queenston, and Princeton Roads then became part of Cleveland Heights.

In the 1910s, Cleveland Heights attracted Cleveland's socially prominent families as Calhoun, the Van Sweringens, and Deming had hoped. In 1915, 34 percent of those listed in the *Cleveland Blue Book* had moved to the suburbs. Nine percent of those families (224) lived in Cleveland Heights; 11 percent (280 families) lived in East Cleveland.[8]

In 1914, however, Calhoun's local real estate empire collapsed; one era had ended, and another had begun. The undeveloped portions of Euclid Heights were sold at sheriff's auctions. Many buyers built single-family homes as gracious as those Calhoun had initially planned. Others built multi-family housing. Handsome apartment buildings soon lined Euclid Heights Boulevard and Hampshire and Overlook Roads. Rows of double homes appeared along Hampshire west of Coventry. The Euclid Club had dissolved, and at Cedar and Fairmount, near the former site of the clubhouse, would be built the Heights Center Building in 1916 and the suburb's first planned shopping center. These varied uses of property originally intended only for suburban millionaires underscored the diverse directions which the suburb had already begun to take.

Most of Cleveland Heights did not become planned enclaves of architecturally distinguished homes, as did the southern section. Instead, the suburb developed as a helter-skelter mix of large country estates, middle-class subdivisions of modest single-family and double homes, clusters of small shops and stores, and old farmhouses. The streetcar tracks, not a realtor's grand vision, provided direction. By 1915, the Euclid Heights streetcar line ran east to Coventry, then north to Mayfield, and as far east as Taylor. In 1918, the Cedar Road streetcar reached Coventry, and in 1922, Lee Road.

Along Noble and Bluestone Roads in the suburb's northern section were farmhouses and barns. Distant from the streetcars, this neighborhood remained almost rural until the 1920s. Quarries had once operated on Bluestone. The names of nearby streets refer to these quarries: Bluestone, Yellowstone, Hillstone, Quarry, Keystone, and Allston. A portion of this area was annexed from South Euclid by Cleveland Heights in the 1920s and became the site of Denison Park.

In contrast, the very wealthy owned huge country estates in the northern section. Rockefeller's Forest Hill spanned the boundaries of East Cleveland and Cleveland Heights. Although he had moved his permanent residence to New York City in 1883, the family maintained a summer home (the ill-fated water cure hotel) in East Cleveland until 1915. The home burned down in 1917. Discussions between Rockefeller and Cleveland Heights officials about developing the huge property began in 1915 and continued for more than two decades.

The Severance family members moved from Euclid Avenue to permanent homes in Cleveland Heights; the Millikins, in 1913; and Elizabeth Severance Allen, recently widowed, in 1915. Both families replaced their summer farmhouses with mansions in English revival styles. The Millikins' was called Ben Brae. Allen, who married Francis Fleury Prentiss in 1917, named her more formal brick home Glen Allen. In 1911, John L. Severance moved to Cleveland Heights across the street from his cousin and sister on the 125-acre parcel purchased by

FARM HOUSES ON BLUESTONE ROAD. These two homes and the barn are reminders of this neighborhood's rural past. (Cleveland Heights Planning Department.)

his father, Louis Henry Severance. After his father died in 1913, John L. Severance inherited this property, which he named Longwood. Architect Milton Dyer designed the first version of his vast Tudor mansion and Charles Schweinfurth, the leading architect for Cleveland's elite, remodeled it. Like his father, John L. Severance had ambitions to develop the area, and in 1910–1911, had begun buying parcels for a subdivision of smaller homes planned for the eastern border of his father's property. In 1915, Severance enlarged his estate to 240 acres by purchasing the 100-acre Minor farm south along Taylor.

As Severance realized, this area was ripe for residential development. Near the Severance estates, developers had already laid out small, gridded subdivisions on streets that ran off Mayfield, Noble, and Taylor. Although these boasted grand names like Compton Estates, Noble Heights, Maple Villa, or Yellowstone Estates, lots were much smaller than those in the southern section of the suburb, and homes were intended for middle-income buyers. Advertisements for Maple Villa and Park Hill Allotment pointed out that they were on the inter-urban route to Gates Mills and close to the streetcar as well ("10 minutes walk from Euclid Heights car"); they boasted that city improvements were already in (sewer, water, gas, sidewalks) and especially that buying property now was a good investment ("only a question of a short time when these values will double").[9]

In general, these subdivisions did not contain architect-designed homes, nor did developers attempt to impose any architectural uniformity. Some homes were

JOHN L. SEVERANCE'S LONGWOOD. This grand country estate was soon surrounded by small subdivisions, one developed by Severance himself. (Cleveland Press Collection.)

simple, modified farmhouses; some were bungalows; some were foursquares with wide porches. Some were copied or adapted from mail order pattern books; several firms, including Sears, Roebuck and Montgomery Ward provided not only the plans but the building materials for houses in popular styles.

Many were two-family homes. From 1915 to 1919, at least a quarter of the homes built in Cleveland Heights were duplexes.[10] Built in all neighborhoods, except for Ambler Heights and the original Euclid Heights allotment, double homes, like the streetcar, made suburban living available to a wide range of the middle class. The Coventry-Mayfield Land Company Allotment built large, gracious double homes, distinguished by their decorative detail, on Coventry, Glenmont, Belmar, Eddington, and Hillcrest Roads, where the streetcar turned east to Taylor. Minor Heights, on the Minor farm immediately west of Taylor and south of Mayfield, was developed by Grant W. Deming, B.R. Deming's brother, as single and double homes. Altamont, Beechwood, Berkeley, and DeSota Roads contained many unpretentious but spacious "Cleveland Doubles," with broad porches and identical first- and second-story apartments.

Although not for the elite, these homes were intended for a respectable middle-class clientele, as indicated by restrictions on the properties. Deeds on lots in the Compton Estates established the price of the homes as not less than $3,000, not including the price of the lot, and also specified the location of the dwelling and any "barn, stable, water closet or other outbuilding." Deeds further stipulated:

"No place of public entertainment nor store, livery stable, or other place of business, nor resort, nor dance hall shall be established. . . . No spirituous, vinous, or fermented liquors shall be manufactured or sold . . . No nuisance shall be caused."[11]

Developers in these middle-income neighborhoods capitalized on the suburb's elite appeal. The Coventry Mayfield Land Allotment Company advertised its subdivision as "a restricted Residential Section, only 32 minutes from the Square, on Euclid Heights Car Line . . . The spot is high, dry, well drained, and [enjoys] refreshing breezes off the lake all summer." The advertisement did not point out that the development was only a few minutes' walk from Little Italy. In 1909, the Forest Hill Allotment near Lee and Superior, also developed by Grant W. Deming, was described in similar terms: "A strictly high-class residence community located in Cleveland's most exclusive residence district in the most desirable section of Cleveland Heights." Within an easy walk were the streetcar, the new high school, the Cleveland Heights Methodist Episcopal Church, the Mayfield Boulevard [Cleveland Heights] Presbyterian Church, and the city hall and fire department, claimed the developer, who also called attention to "the high class character of the

MINOR HEIGHTS DUPLEX. The Minor Heights allotment contained many "Cleveland doubles" with broad porches up and down.

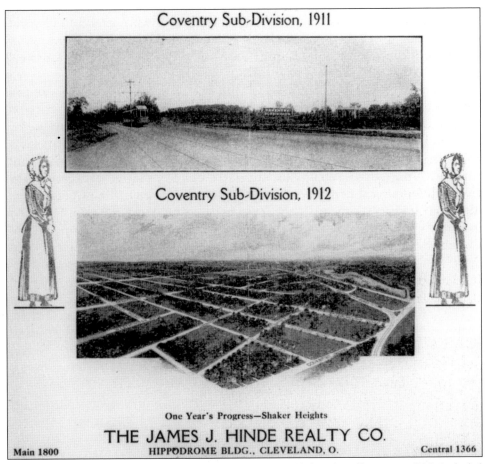

Coventry Sub-Division, 1911

Coventry Sub-Division, 1912

One Year's Progress—Shaker Heights

THE JAMES J. HINDE REALTY CO.

Main 1800   HIPPODROME BLDG., CLEVELAND, O.   Central 1366

COVENTRY SUBDIVISION, 1912. The developer boasted that this allotment, which included Scarborough, Coleridge, Corydon, and Essex, was only a 30-minute streetcar ride to downtown. (Western Reserve Historical Society, Cleveland, Ohio.)

homes in this locality." The development included Lincoln Boulevard, Edgehill, East Overlook, Berkshire, Yorkshire, Parkway, Forest View Drive, and Redwood Roads, where Grant W. Deming's home still stands.[12]

Like homes, commerce followed the streetcar. Shops, stores, and offices were built only in the center section of the suburb, along Lee near Cedar, and in the northern section at Mayfield and Superior near the city hall, on Coventry Road between Euclid Heights and Mayfield, and at Mayfield and Lee, near the Heights Masonic Temple.

Like the other early suburbs of Cleveland, Cleveland Heights grew swiftly: its 1910 population of 2,576 had become 15,264 in 1920. The population of the city of Cleveland had also increased, but less rapidly, to 796,841. Clevelanders spoke dozens of languages, including Polish, Hungarian, German, Russian, and Italian. The first significant immigration of blacks from the impoverished, racially segregated South had also arrived, looking for work in Cleveland's mills and factories. In contrast to Cleveland, Cleveland Heights residents were overwhelmingly white and Anglo-American. Only 12 percent were foreign-born; 45 percent of these had been born in the British Empire.[13]

Despite this ethnic homogeneity, the suburb had gained a small measure of religious diversity. Most church-going residents were Protestant. Cleveland Heights Methodist Episcopal and St. Alban Episcopal Church had been joined by three Presbyterian congregations: Cleveland Heights Presbyterian Church, Noble Road Presbyterian, and Fairmount Presbyterian. However, along the Cedar Road corridor, at the intersection of Coventry and Cedar Roads, Catholics established a beachhead around St. Ann Church. Pastor Father John Mary Powers and interested investors arranged for a loan to the Meadowbrook Land Company from the Cleveland Catholic Diocese. The company then bought property near the intersection, and before the Protestant neighbors could object, Powers established the suburb's first Catholic church in 1915 with parishioners nearby: 180 families in 1917.[14] The surrounding neighborhood contained single homes and clusters of doubles.

The suburb's rapid growth was also illustrated by its thriving school system. Cleveland Heights had inherited three elementary schools from East Cleveland Township: Fairmount (this site was sold in 1910 to the Van Sweringens), Noble, and Superior Schools. In Cleveland Heights's first two decades, residents built a high school, a junior high, four new elementary schools—Fairfax, Lee, Roxboro, and Coventry—and briefly maintained the Severance School, a small facility for children from kindergarten to second grade. In the 1919–1920 school year, 2,942 students attended these public schools, an increase of almost 30 percent over the previous year.[15]

Two events had briefly threatened this growth. The United States' entrance into World War I in April 1917 slowed down home-building because construction materials were scarce. The village council supported the war effort by encouraging residents to plant war gardens in spring 1917 and did some plowing and harrowing of the gardens for a small fee. The Women's Civic Club, formed in 1917, played a more active role in the war effort: buying bonds, conserving food, aiding the Red Cross, and encouraging community gardening.

A more serious threat had emerged in 1916 when residents of the northeastern section of the village, represented by the Noble Heights Civic Club, first approached council with their plans to secede from Cleveland Heights and be re-annexed by East Cleveland. Since no streetcars ran this far east, the neighborhood remained relatively isolated from Cleveland Heights but connected to East Cleveland by Noble and Taylor. Home-owners on the streets north of Mayfield between Taylor and Noble—Nelaview, Greyton, and Selwyn Roads, Helmsdale Drive, and Caledonia Avenue—also pointed out to the Cuyahoga County Board of Commissioners that they paid property taxes to East Cleveland because their neighborhood elementary school, Caledonia, had remained within its school system. Cleveland Heights councilmen opposed the proposed re-annexation and

HIGH SCHOOL FACULTY, 1908. This small but serious group taught the small student body of the first Cleveland Heights High School, built in 1903. (Cleveland Heights-University Heights Board of Education.)

were greatly relieved when the request was turned down by the commissioners in April 1921. The secessionist threat, however, was evidence of disunity within the large suburb, and this neighborhood remained geographically isolated until the 1940s.

This threatened secession and re-annexation had spurred village officials to move quickly to have the Cleveland Heights population counted and the suburb declared a city since this would make the re-annexation more difficult. Realizing that the new city would require a new charter, the village council placed the issue of a new charter and nominees for a charter commission on the ballot in a special election in 1920. Voters approved both. The charter itself was approved by voters in August 1921. It gave the City of Cleveland Heights "home rule," greater autonomy from the state, and new powers that included selling bonds for public projects and letting contracts for public services. Reflecting contemporary efforts to reform local government, the charter provided for nonpartisan elections of the city council and a city manager, who would be chosen by council for his professional expertise. The seven members of Cleveland Heights Council chose the mayor from their own ranks.

The new city's first mayor, Frank C. Cain, was a suburban enthusiast and visionary. He dedicated his three decades in Cleveland Heights politics to realizing his vision. Born in Springfield, Ohio, Cain moved to Cleveland in 1895 and to Cleveland Heights in 1900. Cain was elected a village councilman in 1909 and mayor in 1914, a post he held until 1946. He recalled that his political career grew out of his "ideas for a model city. I wanted a home town that would attract only the best people . . . I wanted streets planned and churches built and beautiful homes erected. I kept on thinking about these things and the first thing I knew I was in politics."[16]

Cain's definition of "the best people" was undoubtedly broader than Calhoun's or Deming's if his own lifestyle is any indication. Cain made his living in the grain and feed business and also dabbled in real estate, developing a block of stores and apartments on Mayfield near the city hall. He lived in the northern section of Cleveland Heights. His homes on Radnor and Compton were substantial and comfortable but not ostentatious (an architect did design the Compton house). His neighbors' tastes in architecture were eclectic rather than elegant; neither street was a grand boulevard. Nevertheless, Cain's vision of a "model city" was not an inclusive one; it certainly did not extend beyond the white middle-class home-owners who were his neighbors, business associates, and political colleagues.

Under Cain's guidance, the council took the first significant step to achieve his vision: effective zoning. Zoning was viewed as an innovative and effective urban planning tool. Without zoning, a city's residential development was dependent upon the good will and the good taste of developers to keep property values high

FIRST CITY HALL. Built in 1909, this dignified building housed all city offices, including the police department. (Cleveland Press Collection.)

and the neighborhoods (and the neighbors) up to the mark. As Cleveland Heights officials knew, not all developers were as fussy as Calhoun, the Van Sweringens, or B.R. Deming. Spurred on by a plea from the Cleveland Heights Civic Club (Cain was a member), council established a Planning and Zoning Commission in 1920. Cain was a member of the commission; so was B.R. Deming. Council then hired a member of the Cleveland Planning Commission who had just drawn up a zoning code for Lakewood to create a code for Cleveland Heights.

The ordinance establishing the code was passed in August 1921. It had one goal: to ensure that Cleveland Heights remained a residential suburb primarily of single-family homes ("most of such restricted [residential] property has been further restricted to single residences"). Cleveland Heights had no industry, but it did have some commerce: the shops and businesses that had grown up along the streetcar lines. Moreover, the suburb had many multi-family homes: apartments in Calhoun's allotment and duplexes throughout the suburb, especially in the Cedar Heights, Minor Heights, and the Coventry-Mayfield Land Company allotment. Clearly, the new zoning code could not change existing land uses. But it could keep less desirable uses from expanding. Such expansion now required permission of the Planning and Zoning Commission. The zoning code did not mandate architectural styles (as would the Van Sweringens in Shaker Heights), but it did acknowledge and reinforce class differences by specifying larger lot sizes in the elite neighborhoods and keeping commerce and multi-family housing out of them. Council hoped that zoning would "preserve the present character" of [the] city.[17]

Early developers had defined Cleveland Heights as a suburb for Cleveland's very well-to-do. As Cain and the council realized, in the two decades since 1901, the reality had become somewhat different. Cleveland Heights had also attracted the merely middle-class. The zoning code, therefore, became a significant strategy for ensuring that the essentials of the initial suburban vision would be maintained: that Cleveland Heights would remain a community with no industry and little commerce whose residents were affluent enough to own and live in single-family homes. This vision continued to attract suburbanites and guide the decisions of city leaders for another half-century.

The zoning code did preserve the physical character of the city, whose infrastructure and land uses have remained substantially unchanged since 1921. The code did not halt the explosive population growth that the suburb was about to experience.

3. Years of Growth
A Suburb Takes Shape(s), 1921–1930

In 1925, Mayor Cain confidently predicted that the city's population would reach 100,000 by 1940. The 1930 census suggested that he was right on target: the suburb had 50,945 residents.[1] Suburbanites and elected officials enthusiastically supported this growth. They bought thousands of homes, opened dozens of shops, formed organizations, and built a city hall, schools, and libraries. Cleveland Heights citizens remained just as enthusiastically committed to the earlier vision of a suburb with connections to the city but aspirations to social exclusivity and political independence. As the decade ended, officials hoped that the long-delayed development of the Rockefeller estate would maintain both the growth and the vision.

Although Cleveland Heights's growth was extraordinary, it was part of a national trend. According to the 1920 census, more Americans lived in cities than elsewhere, but suburbs around the country grew more rapidly than did cities in the next decade. That suburban growth was caused in part by prosperity. After a brief slump in 1920, the economy in urban areas provided a good living for many Americans. Encouraged also by the wide availability of credit, Americans bought as never before: radios, fashionable clothing, tickets to the movies, real estate in Florida, and new homes in suburbia. Developers speculated as energetically in suburban allotments as traders speculated on Wall Street. The expansion of public transit systems and private automobile ownership also hastened the exodus out of American cities.

Cleveland remained the center of the region's industry and commerce. Cleveland had become the second largest center of the automotive industry in the country, home to many manufacturers of automobiles and automotive parts. The city's downtown was bolstered by the construction of the Van Sweringens' $150 million Union Terminal complex on Public Square, the signature structure of Cleveland for five more decades. University Circle, home of Western Reserve University, Case Institute of Technology, and the Cleveland Museum of Art, remained the heart of the area's cultural life. Cleveland's population climbed to more than 900,000 by 1930, but the suburbs of Shaker Heights, Garfield Heights, and Parma, as well as Cleveland Heights, grew 500 percent or more during the 1920s.

The streetcars so crucial to Cleveland Heights's early growth continued to carry its residents downtown on the suburb's major east-west thoroughfares: Mayfield, Euclid Heights, Cedar, and Fairmount. In 1925, the Cleveland Railway Company began bus service north and south on Lee, Taylor, and Noble Roads, encouraging new residential and commercial developments on these streets. By the end of the decade, at the insistent urging of city officials, the railway company extended its line on Euclid Heights, north on Coventry to Mayfield east to Warrensville Center; on Cedar to Lee; and on Fairmount to Canterbury Road. These extensions eliminated "dinkies" (one-car shuttles) and their extra fares on Mayfield from Taylor to Warrensville Center Road and on Washington Boulevard from Coventry to Lee.

Despite the importance of public transportation, Cleveland Heights residents owned and used automobiles for work and pleasure. Once luxury items for the very wealthy, cars, like suburban homes, became the prerogative of middle-class families. Automobiles were a mixed blessing: they made life more convenient but also more dangerous. The *Cleveland Heights Dispatch* regularly headlined automobile fatalities: in June 1926, a six-year-old boy became the suburb's third fatality for the year. In September, the police launched "a crusade against speeding" and arrested 30 speeding motorists in one week, as well as several drunk drivers.[2] Cars also increasingly competed with the streetcars and buses on main

COVENTRY ROAD, C. 1925. *The streetcar and the automobile made this a thriving commercial district and a cluttered thoroughfare. (Western Reserve Historical Society, Cleveland, Ohio.)*

thoroughfares, creating traffic jams. The top of Cedar Glen, Calhoun's gateway to the suburb, became a congested highway. Like buses, automobiles encouraged residential and commercial development along north-south roads and also east of the end of the streetcar lines. Automobiles also changed the appearance of the city. Officials widened Cedar Glen and other main streets. Gas stations opened even in such exclusive neighborhoods as Euclid Heights.

Cleveland Heights housing starts during the 1920s underscored the suburb's dramatic growth. World War I and the brief post-war slump kept the numbers of new family units to 579 in 1920, but from 1922 through 1925, new starts averaged more than 1,200 a year. The boom was big news: the pro-growth *Cleveland Heights Dispatch* carried the number of new building permits on its front page every week. Home-buying was encouraged by easy credit from banks and from developers like Representative Realty, which built many houses in Cleveland Heights. Representative maintained that home-buying "fosters economy and thrift and adds the love of home to the other ties that bind [a home-owner] to the community." Its advertisements pictured homes in a variety of colonial revival styles; prices started at $7,500 for middle-class "wage-earners."[3]

By the end of the 1920s, much of the suburb's residential landscape was almost complete. The elite neighborhoods on the city's south side—Euclid Heights, Ambler Heights, and north and south of Fairmount Boulevard—had filled in. In

AMBLER HEIGHTS HOME, 1917. At the corner of Harcourt and Ambler Parkway, this home overlooked the city of Cleveland. (Case Western Reserve University Special Collections.)

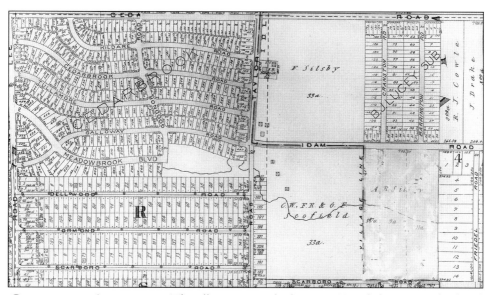

CEDARBROOK ALLOTMENT. The allotment was laid out in 1914 but was not developed until the 1920s when the streetcar went this far east. Dellwood, Ormond, and East Scarborough Roads were also laid out but were almost uninhabited. (Western Reserve Historical Society, Cleveland, Ohio.)

the early apartment house district, handsome buildings on narrow but deep lots with ample front yards lined the north side of Euclid Heights Boulevard between Coventry and Cedar and both sides of Overlook between Kenilworth and Edgehill Road.

Small developers in pursuit of a middle-class clientele continued to build housing along the Cedar Road streetcar line and north and south along Lee and Taylor. John L. Severance began to develop the 100-acre parcel, formerly the Minor farm, as the Severn Park allotment (now Severn, Shannon, and Bendemeer Roads). Although the allotment was "restricted to receive only residential development of the highest class,"[4] its 438 homes were intended for the comfortably well-off, not the very wealthy. The Cedarbrook Allotment, east of Lee and south of Cedar, was also intended for middle-income buyers. The longtime owner of the property, Esther Kneen, had turned over 70 acres (now Kildare, Cedarbrook, and Tullamore Roads) to the J.A. Wigmore Company in 1916. The developers divided the property into lots with 40-foot frontages. Kneen herself lived in one of the allotment's homes on Tullamore until her death in 1928. She saw her farmland become a flourishing residential neighborhood as the nearby Cedar-Lee commercial district grew up.[5] In the northern section of the suburb along Noble, the property of Laura M. Stewart (now Woodview Road) had been subdivided since 1893. A few lots changed hands in 1904, but by the mid-1920s, these 40-foot lots were selling rapidly. So were the small lots of the Rushleigh Subdivision (now Rushleigh, Pembrook, and Yellowstone Roads).

51

ENGLEWOOD BUNGALOW. A formal home displays the versatility of the bungalow style.

PARKWOOD BUNGALOW. Works of art add color and distinction to this traditional bungalow.

In these neighborhoods, bungalows remained popular housing choices. Their owners believed them practical, efficient, yet artistic. Marvelously adaptable to owners' tastes and budgets, bungalows were built in all sizes, all styles, and in all neighborhoods of Cleveland Heights.

Important commercial districts developed at major intersections. Accessible on foot as well as by streetcar and bus, each district served its own well-defined neighborhood. The most architecturally distinctive was a group of eclectic buildings at Cedar and Fairmount near the Heights Center Building. To its north near the former site of the Euclid Golf Club was built the suburb's only residential hotel, the Alcazar, completed in 1923 and intended to evoke southern Europe. On the south side of Fairmount, the three-story C-Fair Building (1926) with cupolas and elaborate exterior stonework, contained offices for professionals as well as a drugstore, hardware, and beauty shop.

The shopping district at Cedar and Lee, where the streetcar met the bus line, became the commercial center of Cleveland Heights, extending several blocks north and south of Cedar along Lee. The district had the suburb's second movie theater, the Cedar-Lee (1926), several restaurants and delicatessens, tailors and clothing stores, a bank, butchers, bakers, two creameries, a gas station, two drugstores, two chain grocery stores, and the offices of music teachers, dance teachers, and the Heights School of Expression and Dramatic Art.

Many years later, two shop-owners remembered this bustling neighborhood. Marie T. Kish in 1923 had opened a dry goods store at Tullamore and Lee that became an exclusive dress and millinery shop: "There were new homes on Tullamore, new businesses coming in . . . A welcome new neighbor was Clark's Restaurant, on the corner of Cedar and Lee. It was a fine family restaurant . . . we used to go and sit at the round table at Clark's every noon and exchange ideas and talk about the progress that was going on." Angelo Chronis, a recent immigrant from Greece, opened his shoe and hat repair shop on Lee near Cedar in 1924: "this neighborhood was a main area for shopping; people used to come from all over . . . The neighborhood was nice—good people." Chronis remained in his shop for 54 years.[6]

The suburb's first movie theater opened on Coventry Road in 1921, just where the Euclid Heights streetcar turned north to Mayfield. Both sides of Coventry were lined with two-story buildings that housed tailors, drugstores, dressmakers, beauty shops, two banks, grocery stores (Kroger's, an Atlantic and Pacific, and a Piggly Wiggly), bakeries, and dairy stores. Above the businesses were offices and apartments.

The suburb's growth could also be measured by the new organizations established, especially by women, for improving their members and the community. These organizations included the Cleveland Heights Round Table, the Kiwanis, the Cleveland Literary Guild, the View Club, the Critique Club, a local chapter of the Woman's Christian Temperance Union, a Women's Democratic Club (the Newton D. Baker Club, named after Cleveland mayor and then secretary of war under Woodrow Wilson), and the Men's and Women's Civic Clubs.

CEDAR-LEE SHOPPING DISTRICT. The busy neighborhood of shops and offices developed at the intersection of the streetcar and the bus lines. Marie Kish's store was next to the bank. (Western Reserve Historical Society, Cleveland, Ohio.)

The most visible of the organizations was the well-established Women's Civic Club. When World War I ended and women had won the vote, the club became interested in educating women voters and invited politicians to address them on public issues. In 1924, members listened to Mayor Cain; Belle Sherwin, president of the National League of Women Voters; and Cleveland city council member Marie Wing. Members also attended board of education meetings and reported back on education issues to the group. They raised funds for college scholarships for outstanding Cleveland Heights High School graduates. The recipient of $200 in 1928 was Martha Wolfenstein, who would become a well-known local poet. The women also raised funds for the planting of hundreds of trees. Aware of the rapid changes the suburb was experiencing, club members began to collect the materials that became the basis for its first history, *The Proud Heritage of Cleveland Heights.*

This decade also re-affirmed Cleveland Heights's identity as an exclusive suburb. Cleveland Heights continued to attract Cleveland's social elite: in 1931, 35 percent of the families listed in the *Cleveland Blue Book* lived in Cleveland Heights, more than in any other suburb. They lived in all neighborhoods, except the farthest northeast section of the suburb, but clustered in the older, elite sections. In 1924, 70 *Blue Book* families lived on Fairmount Boulevard alone.[7] Close to University Circle, Cleveland Heights also was home to Cleveland's cultural elite. When music impresario Adella Prentiss Hughes needed funds to build a concert hall for the Cleveland Orchestra, she went to her neighbors, John D. Rockefeller and John L. Severance. Both contributed. To honor the memory of his wife Elizabeth, Severance donated most of the funds for the orchestra's permanent home, Severance Hall. At Severance's death in 1936, his extensive art collection and half of his estate, Longwood, went to the Cleveland Museum of Art.

Almost 70 percent of Cleveland Heights residents lived in single-family homes in 1930, but the range of home prices was wide. In 1923, a spectacular Beaux Arts mansion on Fairmount sold for $225,000. A Euclid Golf home with ten rooms and servants' quarters could be purchased for $32,000, a duplex in the Cedar-Lee neighborhood, for $17,800, and a four-bedroom home on Quilliams, off Noble, for $8,500.[8]

Regardless of their socioeconomic status, suburbanites had similar aspirations. These are revealed in the real estate ads: access to the city and workplace, yet closeness to nature; less dense housing—preferably single-family homes—on relatively large lots, and upward social mobility. Realtors and developers pointed out the proximity of homes to streetcar lines, especially the Fairmount streetcar,

FAIRMOUNT BOULEVARD HOME, 1921. The most elite street in Cleveland Heights was home to many families listed in the Cleveland Blue Book. *(Case Western Reserve University Special Collections.)*

"Standard"

The Plumbing and Heating in Many
of the Residences in the

Euclid Golf District

Illustrated in this Publication were
Installed by

J. L. Croft & Co.

Estimates Cheerfully Furnished, Repair
Work Promptly Attended To

Cleveland

*EUCLID GOLF
ADVERTISEMENT,
1921. This appeared in
an elegant brochure for
homes in the Euclid
Golf allotment. (Case
Western Reserve
University Special
Collections.)*

and lavished praise on trees, shrubs, and lawns. Advertisements unembarrassedly exploited the suburb's snob appeal. The southern section of Cleveland Heights had always billed itself as elite: "Spring Opening in Euclid Golf. Sale of Few Remaining Lots . . . in this highly restricted and exclusive residence section of 'The Heights.'" Developer B.R. Deming pointed out that his was a "high class development [with] safe and sensible restrictions, accessibility to all parts of the city or Heights." "Restrictions" here referred to the stringent architectural guidelines imposed by Deming. The term was also used to describe homes in other neighborhoods where developers were less strict, but zoning prohibited commerce or double homes. A "tapestry brick" home in the "Fairmount Section" was located "on a street restricted to single homes in an air of refinement and stability." Regardless of the neighborhood, the term always suggested exclusivity. Developments on the north side of town had considerably less cachet but made the most of what their neighborhoods offered. The Potter Estates off Taylor (Edison, Castleton, Boynton, St. Albans, and Radcliffe Roads) were described inaccurately in 1923 as "directly across from . . . the famous residence of John D. Rockefeller." The Shaker Heights Improvement Company, builder of a new home on Inglewood Drive, pointed out that it was located "Opposite the J.L. Severance Estate."[9]

Home-owners were also enamored of the Anglo-American architectural styles that had become identified with upper-middle-class suburban living, styles that suggested their own connections to a revered past. Realtors encouraged this thinking by describing homes as "colonial" or "English, " regardless of the homes' prices or locations. A 12-room Chatfield Drive home off Fairmount with maid's quarters and bath was "English brick," and so was a $17,500 "wonder home" on Blanche Avenue off Taylor. An $11,500 home at Cedar and Taylor was of the "English type"; so was a duplex on Englewood Road. Even more popular, then and now, was the term "colonial": an "exquisite colonial" on Lamberton Road, a "pretty colonial" on Edgehill. Occasionally, the ad was more specific. A Severn allotment home was "Georgian colonial," and one on Berkshire Road, "southern colonial."[10]

These values and social aspirations were reflected and fostered by Cleveland Heights city council. Like their constituents, they vigorously supported both growth and exclusivity. Most of the men elected to council under the 1921 charter were carry-overs from the pre-charter period: Cain, Robert F. Denison, William C. Dunlap, A.W. Ellenberger, W.G. Hildebran, Dr. R.E. Ruedy, and J. Wentworth Smith. They took office in January 1922, and except that Carl W. Brand replaced Ellenberger when he died, they remained on council throughout the decade. All but Dr. Ruedy and Denison, a lawyer, were successful businessmen who commuted to offices downtown.

The 1921 charter stipulated nonpartisan elections to eliminate any rancorous political disagreements. In any case, voters knew that councilmen were enthusiastic Republicans. In 1919, council resolved to name the suburb's first park "Roosevelt Park" in honor of the late President Theodore Roosevelt and to place there a monument to him. The name never took, and this was always called "Cumberland Park" after the street that constituted its eastern boundary. The monument never got built. The suburb's first junior high school was named Roosevelt, however. These Republicans prided themselves on their efficient, business-like approach to running the city: low taxes were a campaign staple. The advertisement for the four incumbents who ran in 1925 pointed to "the splendid record of efficient and disinterested service . . . Continuity of service . . . is highly advantageous to municipal welfare and progress." Their infrequent opponents, like those in 1925, cast themselves in a like mold: "Progressive Business Men . . . who stand for an economical administration and a fair deal."[11]

Perennially elected mayor by his colleagues and clearly the most forceful figure on council, Cain also became a prominent player in Cleveland politics. In 1923, as president of the Cleveland City Club, he refused to introduce Eugene V. Debs at the club's public forum because Debs had recently been released from federal prison where he was serving time for his opposition to the United States' entrance

FRANK C. CAIN. Cain envisioned a residential suburb of single-family homes served by public transportation; this remained his goal from 1909 until his retirement from Cleveland Heights politics in 1946. (Cleveland Press Collection.)

into World War I. In 1924, Cain was elected president of the Cleveland Metropolitan Council, an organization of local government officials.

Like their constituents, city council admired growth, and throughout the decade, worked hard to attract residents. One attraction was the suburb's public park system. In 1915, the city had begun buying properties for a park system along a ravine that extended from Mayfield southeast to Taylor; these had once been the wine farm of Emil Preyer, the quarry of James Haycox, and the orchards of the Minor family. This land was initially used as a public dump to its neighbors' displeasure. But in 1924, council hired A.D. Taylor, a noted local landscape designer, to plan the northern end of the property that became Cumberland Park.

Council also encouraged development by negotiating water, electricity, and gas rates with suppliers. The improvement and maintenance of streets was a never-ending, expensive process, and especially after the automobile, probably occupied more hours of council time than any other matters.

Continued growth was also dependent on good public transportation. Council, especially Cain, engaged in on-going and sometimes contentious negotiations with the Cleveland Railway Company over rates, maintenance of the tracks, safety, frequency of service, and extension of routes, in order to provide Cleveland Heights residents with the best public transportation at the lowest price. "We're out for blood," declared Cain in 1923, demanding that the railway company provide better service to the 24,000 persons who daily rode "packed in [street]cars like cattle" from Cleveland Heights to downtown Public Square. Cain also demanded the eastward extensions of the streetcar although the company did not provide them for another six years.[12]

Council wished to be connected to Cleveland by streetcar but not by a shared form of government: political independence, recently achieved, remained a goal. During the 1920s, Cleveland annexed portions of Euclid Village (1926), Warrensville Township (1927), Brooklyn Heights Village (1927), and a portion of Miles Heights Village (1928). Except for the annexation of the rest of Miles Heights Village in 1931, these were Cleveland's last successful acquisitions. Larger suburbs, especially elite suburbs, could provide their own services to residents and wished to maintain their own political and social identities. Both East Cleveland and Lakewood rejected annexation in the 1910s.

Cleveland Heights officials also rebuffed annexation overtures in the early 1920s, and throughout the 1920s combated plans for regional government advocated by organizations like the Citizens' League of Cleveland. Since 1917, the league had sponsored an amendment to the state constitution that would allow counties home rule—that is, would allow county governments to supercede smaller political entities. The league maintained that the 93 political subdivisions

CITY SERVICE CREW. Cain boasted of the suburb's fine rubbish and garbage collection. (Cleveland Heights Planning Department.)

within Cuyahoga County, with their 800 elective offices and over 10,000 appointive offices and their separate school, water, and streetcar systems, were inefficient, much too expensive, and obstacles to effective urban planning. By the mid-1920s, these advocates of regional government suggested that suburbs could cooperate on issues like transportation but could maintain their own schools and control their own land uses. "Not annexation but cooperation" was the promise of Cleveland City Manager William R. Hopkins in 1924, when he invited representatives of the suburbs to a conference to form "a Greater Cleveland municipal federation." Hopkins was conciliatory and ingratiating: "Let [suburbs] have their own schools, sewers, street cleaning and garbage collection and even their police, but let them help the city in . . . larger duties that affect them" such as public transportation. City dwellers would benefit from their contact with suburban residents, " usually . . . the highest type . . . They are progressive and intelligent, or they wouldn't have moved away from the city's din and confinement."[13]

Such flattery got Hopkins nowhere with Cain (and it can't have done Hopkins much good with Cleveland residents either). Suburban officials remained suspicious, fearing that annexation, not cooperation, was the real motive. In 1925, Cleveland Heights City Manager Harry H. Canfield took the lead in organizing the Suburban League of Cuyahoga County, composed of 36 cities, villages, and townships, to oppose the county home rule amendment. Cleveland Heights council voted unanimously to condemn the amendment. Cain in 1925 declared, "Our people aren't even thinking about annexation. They have the best garbage and rubbish collection in the state. Our other municipal service is equally as good."[14]

By the end of the decade, regional government had won broad support that included not only the Citizens League, but the Cleveland Chamber of Commerce, the *Cleveland Plain Dealer*, and leading civic groups like the League of Women Voters. Cain held out, however, and continued to denounce political change that would give power to "downtown politicians." Annexation was probably not a real threat, and the county home rule amendment did not pass the state legislature until 1933. But opposition to annexation made for good political posturing and provided an opportunity for suburban politicians and residents to set themselves apart from, and above, their urban neighbors.

Nor was Cleveland Heights interested in annexing undesirable property. In 1926, council rejected a request for annexation from citizens in the new University Heights because its zoning code was not "up to the high standard zoning regulations in vogue in Cleveland Heights," and in 1929, council decided unanimously against annexing the whole suburb.[15] Council did annex 160 undeveloped acres in South Euclid, the site of an abandoned bluestone quarry between Belvoir and Monticello Boulevards. First used for a dump, this site later became Denison Park.

Political autonomy was a way of preserving Cleveland Heights as an exclusively residential suburb. So was the new zoning code. In order to preserve the code, city council in 1923 voted funds to support the village of Euclid when its zoning legislation was challenged before the U.S. Supreme Court. The court in *Euclid v. Ambler Realty* (1926) validated Euclid's zoning code in specific and zoning in general as a means of controlling land use. In light of the court's decision, several lawsuits challenging Cleveland Heights's own zoning ordinance were dropped.

Zoning, however, proved a more problematic planning device than council had probably imagined. Some residents criticized the zoning code as too lenient. The *Cleveland Heights Dispatch*, for example, excoriated the "horrible example of zoning practice" illustrated by a row of bungalows on Euclid Heights Boulevard: "the five stunted abodes look very out of place . . . in such a high-classed community and in such a prominent place." (The bungalows are still there.) East Fairfax Road residents in 1921 asked that no more double homes be permitted on their street.[16] More often, however, citizens asked that the code be made more lenient. The Planning and Zoning Commission and council, which had the final say, generally insisted on strict enforcement. Requests to build double homes were often rejected on the grounds that rental properties might be of lower quality than nearby single-family homes. In 1924, the commission turned down a proposal to build a federal marine hospital on Taylor near the Rockefeller estate so that the area would remain available for single-family development. The demands of residents and business owners for more shopping, however, gradually allowed for an expansion of shops and stores along Lee and Noble.

Council took other steps to control commerce, such as legislation that prohibited movies and most shopping on Sundays. Although the movie prohibitions were removed at the behest of the two movie theater operators, the intent of the legislation was to emphasize that the suburb was a place where Sunday was a day of quiet leisure or Christian worship, not work or frivolous recreation.

Sharing their residents' aesthetic and ethnic preferences, city officials planned and designed public buildings that even more emphatically than private homes defined the suburb as an Anglo-American, upper-middle-class residential enclave.

BELMAR ROAD DUPLEXES. *The Coventry-Mayfield Land Company lined Belmar, Eddington, Hillstone, and Coventry Roads with gracious double homes.*

In 1919, when councilmen first contemplated a new city hall, their first choice for its architect was Charles Schweinfurth, designer of homes for the Severances and other Euclid Avenue families. The war postponed the new building, however, and the architect finally chosen was not Schweinfurth, but William R. Powell. (Powell had also been the architect for Cain's Compton Road home.) Very possibly, Schweinfurth's fees were too high and his tastes too elegant for a suburban public building. Powell's city hall, completed in 1924 on the site of the first city hall, was a simple but imposing, two-story brick structure. Its only ornamentation was a clock tower and the handsome stonework surrounding the front entrance. The *Heights Press* described it: "a colonial structure somewhat reminiscent of Independence Hall at Philadelphia . . . peculiarly appropriate to Cleveland Heights."[17] After the building opened, Powell explained the aesthetic principles that guided the city fathers and himself were based on "the architecture of New England . . . during the Colonial period of our country."[18] Powell expressed these principles in Cumberland Bath House (1927) and two fire stations (1929 and 1931). All three were simple in design but had stonework and handsome slate roofs that represented restrained Anglo-American affluence.

The school board built with a more lavish hand although within the same architectural tradition. The school population had grown even more rapidly than

CITY HALL, 1924. Its architect William R. Powell likened this building to Independence Hall in Philadelphia. This doorway is now the entrance to Honda Motorcars. (Cleveland Public Library.)

Boulevard School, 1924. This elementary school with elaborate decorative detail and two minarets announced the importance of education and the affluence of the new suburb. (Cleveland Heights-University Heights Board of Education.)

the population as a whole, increasing more than 25 percent from 1920 to 1921 alone.[19] The school district quickly added new buildings for Roxboro (1921) and Noble (1922) Schools and new elementary schools in the city's north and central neighborhoods: Taylor (1923), Boulevard (1924), Oxford (1925), and Canterbury (1927). Roxboro Junior High moved out of the elementary school into its own building. Taylor, Boulevard, and Coventry Schools were designed in the "Tudor Gothic" style popular for both schools and colleges during the 1920s. Taylor had fine appointments, such as an auditorium that seated 500 students beneath leaded glass windows. Roosevelt Junior High moved into the old high school when the new Cleveland Heights High School was completed in 1926 at Cedar and Lee. This building boasted a cupola and clock tower and imposing turrets that rose above the dignified three-story brick building, adding an imposing public presence to the commercial intersection. Canterbury School and Monticello Junior High (1930), designed by John R. Graham, were more restrained.

Elementary schools also housed the first libraries. When separate structures were built, they were also done in American colonial and English-derived styles, such as the first main library, designed by Graham, which opened in 1926 at Coventry and Euclid Heights.

Public rituals also celebrated this Anglo-American heritage. The most lavish of these was the annual Fourth of July celebration. This featured fireworks, a pageant, and a concert, often on the Rockefeller estate.

BASKETBALL IN BLOOMERS, 1922. The high school team demonstrated the importance of women's athletics. (Cleveland Heights-University Heights Board of Education.)

At the end of the decade, however, home-building, the symbol and engine of suburban growth and prosperity, dropped off sharply: 583 new units in 1928 and only 295 in 1929.[20] But help was at hand. The largest single piece of Cleveland Heights property, Rockefeller's Forest Hill allotment, was at long last to be developed.

Since 1915, city officials had been in discussion with Rockefeller about his plans for the property. Although Rockefeller's summer home had been in East Cleveland, much of the estate, clearly intended for development, was in Cleveland Heights. Plans for the residential development of this portion of the estate were far enough along in 1921 that they appeared on the zoning map. But city officials and the Rockefeller family could not agree about the exact location of Monticello Boulevard. The city wanted to run the boulevard through the Rockefeller property, hoping that Monticello would become the north side's version of Fairmount Boulevard, an elite thoroughfare with a streetcar. The boulevard would also connect the Taylor and Noble neighborhoods more directly with the Mayfield streetcar line and open up for further development this distant section of the suburb.

In 1925, plans for a $60-million residential community of 600 homes on a portion of the estate were finally unveiled by the Rockefeller interests. B.R. Deming, the creator of the Euclid Golf allotment, was to be the developer. The community was to contain both very expensive and middle-income housing, set on winding roads and landscaped grounds: "a gem set in the heart of suburban

Cleveland, finer even than [the] Euclid Golf [allotment] . . . because more carefully planned and regulated." Moreover, the *Heights Press* commented, the Rockefeller development would improve "the whole tone . . . in the entire eastern end of Cleveland Heights and [check] certain isolated tendencies toward inferior development."[21] For the next four years, however, the city and Rockefeller representatives apparently could not resolve their disagreements, most importantly over Monticello Boulevard. In the meantime, the Rockefellers entertained other prospects, including a suburban campus for Western Reserve University.

At last, on October 7, 1929, after 14 years of negotiations between the oil titan and the suburb and four years of enthusiastic speculation by the local press, the Rockefeller plat was finally accepted by city council. The sheer scope of the development was breath-taking, proof to Cleveland Heights citizens and officials of the imagination and power of this richest man in the world and former neighbor.

DETAIL, CLEVELAND HEIGHTS HIGH SCHOOL, 1926. The impressive entrance to the high school, accentuated by the vertical turrets and clock tower, is masked by a later addition. (Cleveland Heights– University Heights Board of Education.)

As in the earlier elite developments, the streets would bear historic English names and be laid out in graceful curves. But this development would be different in significant ways. First, it was much larger and was intended to be a self-contained community, complete with a commercial section and apartments. The neighborhood was to be anchored by a handsome commercial and office building, the Heights Rockefeller Building. Designed by New York architect Andrew Jackson Thomas, and now listed on the National Register of Historic Places, this would be "the most beautiful business development in Cleveland Heights . . . even more beautiful" than Shaker Square, the elegant shopping center that served the Van Sweringens' Shaker Heights.[22]

Second, although the street names were English—Newbury and Chelsea Drive, Brewster, Rumson, Kew, and Burlington Roads—the proposed architecture was not "English" or "colonial" but French Norman, the newest fashion in suburban design. Shaker Heights, then at the zenith of its popularity as an elite suburb, boasted many French Norman homes, but Cleveland Heights had very few.

The developers planned to use only a few home models, placed in pairs that would be mirror images of each other. Third, this was a post-automobile development, bounded by north-south streets, Lee and Taylor. All homes were to have attached garages. Fourth, the Rockefeller development would be even more exclusive than the southern section of Cleveland Heights: the sale of these properties to Jews or African Americans was limited by deed restrictions. The model for these racially restrictive covenants may have been those imposed by the Van Sweringens in Shaker Heights.

As had Cleveland Heights's first two decades, the Rockefeller development revealed the contradiction between the vision of an exclusive suburb and the economic imperatives of suburban growth. The Rockefellers hoped to sell many more homes than had any previous developer; their plans made Calhoun, Deming, and the Van Sweringens look like small stuff. But how to maintain the exclusivity of 600 homes and their buyers?

The uniformity of the housing and the racially restrictive prohibitions on the properties were the Rockefeller answers to this question. Cain and his council had faced a similar dilemma: how exclusive can a suburb of 100,000 people be? For them, however, there was no easy answer. Even with the zoning code, Cain and his council could do little to control the growth they encouraged, and the suburb and its residents had developed in ways that city officials could not have imagined.

In early 1930, despite the sharp downturn in the stock market, Cleveland Heights had promising prospects. The first Rockefeller homes had been built, and the Heights Rockefeller Building was completed. The Van Sweringens had promised improved railway service by running streetcars underground. New development was in store for the Cedar-Fairmount commercial district, although this would necessitate the destruction of B.R. Deming's own home. The board of education finished Monticello Junior High; two new schools were on the drawing boards. The city began to turn the dumpsite at Taylor and Superior into the park that in 1934 would be named for Mayor Cain.

But Cleveland Heights never achieved 100,000 residents. None of the proposed apartment buildings and only 81 of the Rockefeller homes were finished. Only a dozen of these were in Cleveland Heights, and the rest were in East Cleveland. The Van Sweringens' real estate and railroad empires went bankrupt. The two new schools would not be built for another decade and a half. Cain Park would be completed with federal money. B.R. Deming's house still stands. With the rest of the country, Cleveland Heights faced its first great emergency, the Great Depression.

ROCKEFELLER HOMES. The development of handsome, uniform French Norman homes is listed on the National Register of Historic Places.

4. NATIONAL EMERGENCIES HIT HOME
DEPRESSION AND WAR, 1930–1946

In April 1931, a local magazine praised Cleveland Heights as "an almost perfectly planned city," waxing enthusiastic about its police department and garbage collection, its growing tax base, and its small debt.[1] At the very least, the comment was ill-timed. Those services were soon cut and tax revenues dwindled as the city's finances became imperiled by the onset of the Great Depression. During its duration, city officials and residents worked hard to provide for those in need, although ultimately the New Deal shouldered most of this responsibility. The entrance of the United States into World War II brought a return to financial stability and an opportunity for Cleveland Heights men and women to serve their community and their country. Both the Depression and the war changed the community: they irretrievably altered the private lives of citizens and shook the community's belief that a suburb could escape the problems of the larger world.

Even before the great stock market crash of October 1929, Cleveland's booming economy had begun to fade as the buying of automobiles and other heavy durable goods slowed. The Van Sweringens' Terminal Tower was dedicated in 1930. Within months, tens of thousands of Clevelanders were out of work, and the Van Sweringens were bankrupt. The Depression had begun in earnest. Thousands of homeless men wandered the city streets. The unemployed and under-employed competed for scarce, low-paying public works jobs in Cleveland parks. Hungry families lined up for surplus food distributed by local charities.

Despite its middle-class population, Cleveland Heights felt the impact of the Depression almost immediately. In October 1930, only a year after the Rockefeller plans had promised growth and prosperity, 91 lots in John L. Severance's exclusive Severn Park allotment were sold at auction. Cleveland Heights, like Shaker Heights and University Heights, initiated small public works projects that hired residents to clean up parks and repair sewers.

Americans were encouraged by President Herbert Hoover to believe that this business downturn would be short-lived and that local governments and private charity could relieve needy neighbors, as they had in the past. Consequently, during 1931, as the economy worsened, Cleveland Heights officials and residents continued to improvise with stop-gap measures to provide work and help. In April 1931, the city sponsored a "spring clean up" which urged residents to hire unemployed neighbors; its slogan was "Work to Do—Men to Do It—Start Now." Such work relief did not help all those in need. Teachers and students at Cleveland Heights High School collected donations for Thanksgiving baskets for needy families.

Both city council and the board of education began a series of belt-tightening measures that continued for almost a decade. In 1931, council hoped to trim the 1932 budget by cutting back on street repairs and other services; the school board, by reorganizing the school administration. The city saved $1,000 by not sponsoring the annual Fourth of July fireworks display, deciding that the money would better be spent supplying unemployed men with jobs. In place of this community ritual, the American Legion sponsored athletic events at the high school and Cumberland Park. Thanks to low tax collections, the city ended 1931 with a frighteningly small cash balance, although city officials maintained that the city remained financially viable.

Residents faced harder times as the Depression deepened. In response, in February 1932, the school board instituted "depression lunches" for schoolchildren, who received "healthy helpings" of macaroni and cheese, escalloped potatoes, or liver and bacon for 12¢ to 15¢. Both the city and the school board continued to trim their budgets. But in July, facing unprecedented

RESERVOIR AT TAYLOR AND SUPERIOR, 1931. This reservoir may have been one of the city's efforts to provide public works jobs to unemployed residents. (Cleveland Press Collection.)

CUMBERLAND POOL, 1932. The new public pool was a popular place during the Depression when the season's attendance sometimes approached 100,000. (Cleveland Public Library.)

difficulties, city council cut some services, such as waste paper collection and slashed all city salaries 20 percent in an effort to balance the budget. Teachers got a 10 percent salary cut shortly afterwards. The city also continued relief measures that included providing community gardens for schoolchildren and allowing unemployed men to cut up trees in the park for firewood.

By late 1932, when it had become apparent that the economic downturn was going to be longer and more severe than anyone had first thought, the city developed a system of caring for its needy that combined public works and private direct relief. City manager Harry C. Canfield oversaw the system. Voters had passed a $25,000 bond issue in November, which allowed the city to put unemployed men to work improving the city's parks. As the year ended, however, "the city was confronted with a greater increase in the number of families who were in great distress." The solution was to provide men with only two weeks of work each month, making work relief funds available to more families. The city employed a special investigator to determine the "worthiness" of each work recipient. In January 1933, 165 men were so employed, receiving $3.20 a day or about $41 a month for two weeks' work. Work relief was never enough, however, and in any case, not all unemployed residents were able-bodied men who could work outdoors. In fall 1932, therefore, 36 private organizations, including the

Women's Civic Club, had established the Welfare Group of Cleveland Heights to provide direct relief—food, fuel, clothing, and medical assistance—to the suburb's residents. Goods were collected by the group and distributed by Canfield. In January 1933, 110 families received such direct relief from the city. Canfield made a rather murky distinction between these families and those living elsewhere. The Cleveland Heights needy, he explained, "were in dire distress not because of conditions which apply to a great many families in the city of Cleveland and elsewhere, but because of the unusual condition existing throughout the country by reason of lack of employment through no fault of their own." In addition, some Cleveland Heights families were aided by Cleveland Associated Charities and the Jewish Social Service Bureau; the city compensated these agencies for their relief services.[2]

Throughout the decade, Canfield remained in charge of the suburb's relief efforts. A Cleveland native, a graduate of Western Reserve University, and the son of one of Cleveland's leading physicians, Dr. Martha Canfield, he had been chosen clerk of council in 1910, and in 1921, he became the suburb's first city manager. His department was responsible for hiring all city personnel, letting contracts for city improvements, purchasing city equipment, and maintaining city

NOBLE ROAD STORES, C. 1935. Farmview and Baetz were local chain stores; Farmview's prices indicate how far a dollar went during the Depression. (Cleveland Heights Planning Department.)

properties. He was particularly interested in parks and recreation and had personally overseen the building of the Cumberland Park pool and bathhouse. After 1933, Canfield also served as the city's liaison to county and federal relief agencies.

In 1933, the fiscal problems of both the city and the school board were compounded by the collapse of local banks, where public funds remained frozen. Consequently, teachers and other public employees often bore the brunt of the economic collapse. Teachers took another pay cut in February and in March received only 50 percent of their salaries. Although better off than teachers in Shaker Heights, who briefly received no paychecks, Cleveland Heights teachers, who only three years earlier had collected food for the needy, now found themselves in serious financial difficulty. "Many teachers," according to the *Heights Press*, reported that "they have had their phones disconnected and have given up their rooms or apartments and have moved in with relatives or with other teachers."[3] Public library staff also got their salaries cut. In spring, the city added several acres to its gardens for the unemployed, anticipating twice as many jobless men and their families. In May, the Welfare Group launched its third food drive in seven months. It had distributed to more than 100 needy families, 8,396 articles of food, 325 sacks of wheat, 521 sacks of flour, and 159 tons of coal since February, and the group's cupboards were bare.[4]

By the end of 1933, some desperately needed help came from President Franklin D. Roosevelt's New Deal. Its Civil Works Administration (CWA) took some Cleveland Heights men off the city's work relief rolls and paid them to

EUCLID HEIGHTS AND COVENTRY, 1934. Coventry School children cheerfully dashed across this intersection, heedless of the traffic and the Depression. (Cleveland Heights-University Heights Board of Education.)

work on the city parks and streets. The CWA's first project was widening and landscaping Cedar Glen. The *Heights Press* breathed a sigh of relief: "Thanks to the CWA, plus an alert city administration, . . . scores of families are changed from the pittance of charity to the more liberal relief payrolls of CWA."[5]

Even so, 1934 was a terrible year. The suburb's expenditures on relief had risen from $485 in 1930 to $77,163 in 1933, although its net expenditures had dropped by almost 40 percent.[6] Clearly, this spending could not continue, especially as tax revenues continued to decline. In February, in the face of CWA cutbacks, Cleveland Heights, one of the few suburbs that still funded its own work relief program, relinquished it to the Cuyahoga County Relief Administration, the newly created pass-through agency for all federal and other public relief funds. Cleveland Heights continued its own privately funded direct relief program for residents not eligible for county funds. In November, voters turned down special operating levies for the city and the schools. The school board was forced to close the schools for a month rather than two weeks at Christmas.

For the next three years, federal public works programs kept the city and its residents afloat. The new federal Works Progress Administration (WPA) provided more substantial aid than the CWA. The city requested and received funds for a laundry list of street and curb repairs and street-widening; the city paid some of the costs. At the end of 1935, Cleveland Heights was awarded 12 projects totaling $178,000 for street improvements and painting the interiors of public buildings. City employees had their pay cuts restored. In January 1936, the WPA pledged $800,000 in more public works that would put 600 men to work, mostly

HEIGHTS HIGH SCHOOL CONCERT BAND, 1936. Despite cuts in teachers' salaries, the school system developed an excellent musical education program. (Cleveland Heights Planning Department.)

resurfacing streets. In August, however, voters turned down a levy that would have allowed city council to increase the city's debt without a special election. To balance the budget, city council cut services further. In November 1937, there were an estimated 685 Cleveland Heights residents out of work, a larger percentage of the population than in Shaker Heights, but a smaller percentage than in Lakewood and East Cleveland.[7]

Again, the Rockefeller interests came to the rescue, at least indirectly, by giving Cleveland Heights and East Cleveland in 1938 the undeveloped portion of the family estate for Forest Hill Park. This gift had been Cain's dream for almost two decades. The Rockefellers paid for a survey of the park, and the park in turn provided WPA jobs for hundreds of Cleveland Heights residents.

The housing industry revealed the devastating path of the Depression. From 1932 to 1938, 1,164 Cleveland Heights homes were foreclosed and sold at sheriff's auctions. Most homes were on the moderately priced streets of northern Cleveland Heights, but residents in all neighborhoods, even on Fairmount Boulevard, lost their homes. During the same period, however, almost as many new homes—1,043—were built. In 1938, there were 272 housing starts; almost as many as in 1930.[8]

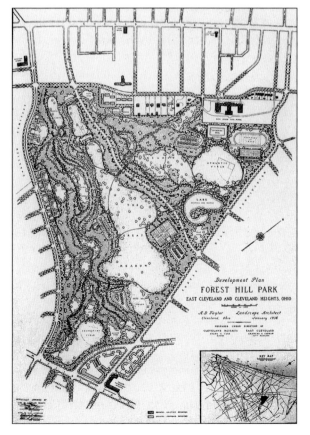

FOREST HILL PARK, 1938. This was the original plan for the parklands donated by the Rockefeller family to the cities of Cleveland Heights and East Cleveland. (Case Western Reserve University Special Collections.)

WPA PROJECT, FOREST HILL PARK. The federal government put unemployed men to work widening the roads in the park. (Cleveland Press Collection.)

By 1939, the worst of the Depression was over for Cleveland Heights. The suburb did not join other municipalities in an effort to create a centralized relief agency. Cain explained that Cleveland Heights "would soon find itself spending money to provide relief for other communities . . . [S]ince relief in the city has been well taken care of in the past . . . there could be no good reason for a change."[9] At the close of the year, home construction was up, and the city's indebtedness was low. In spring 1940, improvements to Forest Hill Park and Cain Park became the last significant federal public works project in the suburb.

The federal government spent well over $2 million in Cleveland Heights, probably due to the city's own record of fiscal prudence, the efforts of the city manager, and the help of U.S. Representative Chester Bolton, a friend of Cain's and a fellow Republican.[10] The New Deal left a generous legacy to Cleveland Heights: a widened, landscaped Cedar Glen; the stonework, tennis courts, a shelter, promenade, and backstage building in Cain Park; walled-up creeks and playgrounds in Forest Hill Park; a WPA mural at Oxford School; a widened Monticello Boulevard; and countless improved streets.

Cain himself remained fervently Republican and a bitter foe of Franklin D. Roosevelt. Soliciting and accepting New Deal money was a practical matter in which personal political preferences had to take a back seat to the public good. According to his daughters, when Roosevelt appeared in newsreels at the local movie theater, Cain " would stand up, turn his back to the screen and say in a loud

WPA PROJECT, MONTICELLO BOULEVARD. The New Deal's Works Project Administration widened Monticello Boulevard. (Cleveland Heights Planning Department.)

voice, 'I don't want to see that damn fool.' "[11] (Cain did not press his earlier suggestion that Cumberland Park be named Roosevelt Park.)

Neither did Cleveland Heights voters seem grateful for New Deal help, for they consistently voted Republican in national elections, going very narrowly for presidential candidate Alf Landon in 1936 and more enthusiastically for Wendell Willkie in 1940. City council also remained solidly Republican. Council membership also remained unchanged, except that senior member J. Wentworth Smith retired. Smith, the contractor and builder of the mansions of John L. Severance and Elizabeth Severance Prentiss, had served on council since 1904. He was replaced by longtime school board member William L. Eggers. Council's philosophy also remained unchanged throughout the decade. Low taxes and low debt remained political principles even if these cost jobs and public services during hard times.

As in the matter of shared relief efforts, council remained committed to suburban autonomy. Cain again played a leading role. After the state amendment permitting county government finally passed in 1933, Cain unsuccessfully ran his own slate of candidates for the commission that was to write the new county charter. In 1935, he opposed the very weak form of metropolitan government that the charter commission finally created. In 1936, however, the State Supreme Court invalidated this new charter. As they had earlier, advocates of metropolitan government argued that it would be more efficient and economical, a compelling argument in these times of financial difficulty. As he had before, Cain maintained that he already ran an economical, efficient suburb and that metropolitan government was another name for annexation. Cain had the support of some suburban newspapers like the *Heights Press*, but a majority of residents voted for both the amendment and the county government.

The Depression and the New Deal had touched almost all Cleveland Heights residents in some way. Heights citizens led Greater Cleveland's relief efforts. Bell Greve directed the Cuyahoga County Relief Board from 1937 to 1944 and later became director of the city of Cleveland Department of Health and Welfare, the second woman to serve in a mayor's cabinet. A.V. Cannon served *pro bono* as head of the Cuyahoga County Relief Agency. Hundreds of residents had worked on the city's streets and parks, sustained by the CWA and the WPA. Hundreds had received direct relief from the city and the federal government. Small businesses like Heights Bakery, Nick's Barber Shop, Foster Frocks, and Nela View Delicatessen and Creamery had enthusiastically displayed the Blue Eagle of the short-lived National Recovery Administration. Cain Park, despite its namesake's Republican politics, had hosted Federal Theater Productions.

Decades later, many residents had vivid memories of these hard times. "People didn't have any money," remembered Howard Drexler, whose father, Leroy Dreschler, had a drugstore at Mayfield and Lee: "Guys that were on the WPA didn't have enough money to buy milk for their babies or children . . . and my father would run a tab for these people knowing that they would get paid so much per month and they were all hard working people. Eventually they got themselves straightened out; I don't think we ever got stuck for a nickel." Wives like Mrs.

CAIN PARK TENNIS COURTS. Cain Park, as well as Forest Hill Park, benefitted from WPA funds. (Cleveland Heights Planning Department.)

Armen Evans, whose husband built their home on Meadowbrook Boulevard in 1931, stretched the family dollars to the breaking point: "I told my husband many times, 'By golly, I have to sew something on this darn coat just about every night!' I kept it together with my needle and thread . . . I used to wonder when the day would come that I would have more than one dress to wear to a PTA meeting." These economic difficulties made the class differences between residents more apparent. In 1932, Sam and Sadie Russo opened their grocery store at Fairmount and Cedar near the Euclid Heights, Ambler Heights, and Euclid Golf neighborhoods. They remembered that their customers "were blue-blood people; elite people. The Depression didn't seem to affect them." William McCarthy, who delivered the milk for Dean Dairy in these neighborhoods, recalled that their residents "didn't have too many inconveniences . . . They had so many maids . . . They'd have a cook, they'd have an upstairs maid, then they'd have girls to come in and help clean, they'd have one to two chauffeurs . . . Rolls Royces were a dime a dozen."[12]

In 1940, the effects of the Depression lingered; Cleveland Heights was still carrying 36 families on direct relief.[13] But the city's population had grown 10 percent since 1930 despite the hard times and in 1940 stood at just under 55,000. Cleveland Heights became the 11th largest city in Ohio. The village of University

CEDAR-FAIRMOUNT SHOPPING DISTRICT, 1940. The Russos had already opened their grocery store, served by both the Cedar and the Fairmount streetcar lines. (Western Reserve Historical Society, Cleveland, Ohio.)

Heights became a city in 1940, and in 1942, Cleveland Heights and University Heights merged their school systems.

The outbreak of World War II brought further changes. Class differences were diminished, and the antipathy for the Roosevelt administration was lessened by an effort that engaged and unified the community in unprecedented ways.

In September 1940, as the European conflict escalated, Congress initiated the nation's first peacetime draft. "The 'draft toll' will be felt for the first time in Shaker and Cleveland Heights homes, neighborhoods, churches and corner stores," announced the *Heights Press* on January 31, 1941. Eighty-four men were required to report to the Central Armory for induction into the Army.

By spring 1941, Heights women's organizations had sprung into action. They rolled bandages, knitted layettes, collected clothes, and raised funds for war relief as they had during the First World War. The mayors of Shaker, University, and Cleveland Heights proclaimed Saturday, July 19 as "Aluminum Pick-Up Day," urging the 80,000 residents of the three suburbs to collect "pots, pans, aluminum toys, parts of vacuum cleaners" and bring them to collection depots.[14]

When the United States formally entered the war on December 8, 1941, after the bombing of Pearl Harbor, Cleveland Heights, like the rest of the country, threw itself whole-heartedly behind the war effort. Heights men rushed to join the armed forces. The three local recruiting stations were crowded with "young men begging to be sent to the front immediately, some of them accompanied by parents, some by sweethearts, but mostly they [were] alone and determined to get an early opportunity to serve Uncle Sam," exclaimed the *Heights Press* on January 2, 1942. Every week for the next four years, the front page of the *Heights Press* published the names and sometimes the photographs of those reporting for military service. "These young men come from established families in this community . . . The Heights honors them and their families at this time when the fate of liberty-loving nations can well be at stake and in the hands of these young citizens," maintained the paper. Some who served were well-known community figures, like Clinton A. Drury, who was on the high school faculty, or Cameron C. Elliott, recently married and captain of the 1936 high school basketball team. Most names were familiar only to family, friends, and neighbors: R.H. Rudolph, Cain's neighbor on Compton; R.F. Spada of Mayfield; or the three sons of the S. Howard Benz family—William, Howard, and John Henry "Jack."[15]

The paper also reported in its column, "The Bugle Call," news of men in training camps, overseas, and home on leave. "It won't be long now until two more Heights men receive their commissions as lieutenants at Foster Field in Texas. Both Gordon Prentice [of] Monticello Boulevard, and Walter J. Goodman, [of] Middlehurst Road are slated for these honors," the paper recorded on June 5, 1942. On November 20, 1942, the paper congratulated Lieutenant Robert N. Seaver, 22-year-old son of Mr. and Mrs. Charles H. Seaver of Lincoln Boulevard, for winning his silver wings and his second lieutenant's commission.

The city administration enlisted all public institutions in the war effort. Within weeks, the police department, under Canfield's direction, was training air raid

THE HIGH SCHOOL GOES TO WAR, 1942. High school girls sponsored "Uncle Sam's Recruiting Station" to encourage participation in the war effort. (Cleveland Heights-University Heights Board of Education.)

wardens, a civil defense committee was appointed, and Cain suggested tags for children that would identify them in the event of an air raid. The city placed in strategic locations piles of sand that could be used as protection against bomb fires. In April 1942, the city boasted of the "best civilian defense" in the county and in July ran a civil defense drill that involved "1,466 air wardens, 552 messengers, 216 Boy Scouts, 244 fire watchers, 119 auxiliary police, 73 auxiliary firemen, 74 medical aides, 23 [persons] at rescue squads, 33 at the report center, 16 regular police and 25 regular firemen."[16] Cain Park Theater extended its 1942 season to raise morale. The season included an original drama, *Army Red*, which portrayed an air raid on Cleveland Heights to show how citizens were supposed to respond. In August, the park hosted a "Victory Sing" with the Cleveland Heights Symphony Orchestra that was also broadcast on the radio, and in summer 1943, an interfaith worship service.

Schools also went to war. The high school formed a Central War Council to arouse patriotism and preparedness. The high school machine shop was used to train workers for defense jobs, and the building itself became an emergency shelter. Plans for a new elementary school were still on hold, but in 1942, teachers got their full pay for the first time in a decade.

Private citizens had ample opportunities to contribute to the war effort. In spring 1942, veterans' groups organized two public send-offs for inductees, complete with chicken dinners and pie a la mode. Hundreds of residents served as air raid wardens and on the draft and ration boards, and many planted victory gardens. They donated generously to the "Buy a Bomber for [Douglas] MacArthur" campaign and to Red Cross fund drives; they bought millions of dollars' worth of war bonds. Citizen participation was doubtless encouraged by graphic advertisements, such as the one that portrayed Hitler and a swastika-bearing flag and urged citizens to buy war stamps and bonds to "MAKE SURE Hitler will never reach our City Hall."[17]

As it did across the country, the war provided special opportunities for local women. Some joined the 350,000 women who served in all branches of the armed services. The *Heights Press* published their names and photos on its front pages, just as it did the men's. On December 4, 1942, the weekly hailed Elsie Linden, who had joined the WACS after being a secretary for 13 years. On January 25, 1945, the paper published photos of a dozen women in uniform—" 'women in blue' in the world's greatest Navy." These included Yeoman M.W. Haggerty of Demington Drive, Ensign R.G. Anderson of Lynn Park Drive, and Specialist First Class J. Keiffer of Selwyn Road. On April 5, 1945, the paper honored women in the Marine Corps: Helen A. Russell of Dresden Road, Ellen E. Summerhill of Montford Road, Virginia McConlogue of Washington Boulevard.

Women also fought on the home front. In 1943, the *Heights Press* advertised for female defense workers—"Girls and Women, Defense plant, opportunities in light electrical assembly . . . Women needed for War Work, Light Assembly, Coil Winders"; photographs of patriotic "Heights Women in War Work" appeared.[18] Women organized dozens of block groups that united residents in neighborhoods across the city in the collection of scrap metal, old clothes, and paper, the sale of war stamps and bonds, the raising and canning of food, and other war-time activities. In 1944, the Rexwood block collected 1,185 pounds of tin cans, 171 pounds of waste fat, 2.5 tons of newspapers, and 335 pounds of old clothing; 18 residents on the block had donated blood.[19] Director of the Block Plan was Mrs. Howard Whipple Green. Green, twice past president of the Women's Civic Club, also organized the city's seven war bond drives, which enlisted hundreds of other women. All drives surpassed their ambitious goals.

In *Memoirs of an Ex-Prom Queen*, Alix Kates Shulman, who grew up in Cleveland Heights, described her own family's war-time efforts. " [W]e collected the foil inner wrappers of chewing gum, chocolate bars, and cigarette packs, which themselves all became scarcer and scarcer until they too, like the Cheshire Cat, finally disappeared entirely. We lived instead on the sweets of patriotism . . . My father, an energetic attorney, sat on the Draft Board, making our family eligible for a prestigious B-card, which entitled us to an extra monthly ration of gasoline, and weekly donned his Air Raid Warden's helmet. My glamorous mother rolled her own cigarettes using begged tobacco, served meat substitutes without complaining, and set up a cozy blackout shelter in the basement of our house."[20]

As Shulman recalled, the war brought inconveniences. Sugar, coffee, red meat, processed foods, and shoes were rationed. So were gasoline, tires, and new automobiles. The city cut back on rubbish collection to save gasoline and rubber. Garbage cans filled up as city laborers briefly went on strike.

The war also brought tragedy and heartbreak. On September 11, 1943, Lieutenant Robert N. Seaver's photograph appeared again. He had already become a casualty. So had Walter Goodman and 57 other Heights men; 13 were missing in action. Twenty-one Cleveland Heights men were listed as prisoners of war on July 6, 1944. By Christmas 1944, 97 Cleveland Heights families had lost sons. In August 1945, just as the war with Japan ended, Mrs. Ralph Morris received official word that she had lost her second son, Robert J. Pringle, 22, in an aircraft crash in India; her older son, Lieutenant David Pringle, 24, had died in France five months earlier.[21] War respected no class; these young men had lived in all the city's neighborhoods, rich and poor.

When the fighting ended, the armed forces rapidly demobilized. Cleveland Heights men and women returned to homes and families, to old jobs or new opportunities created by the GI Bill. The block organizations were disbanded. Rationing was slowly relaxed. But like the Depression, the war left a tangible legacy. At the northern end of Cumberland Park stands a small building of stone and wood to honor those who served in this war, the World War II Memorial, designed by Samuel K. Popkins and William R. Powell. Behind glass panels are the names of these 5,400 men and women. Gold stars mark the names of 191 men who would never return to their families, their neighbors, and their community.

The end of the war also marked the end of a political era. For as the conflict overseas wound down, the suburb's first significant political conflict at home heated up. In June 1945, Cain announced that he would not be a candidate for re-election in November after 24 years as mayor and 35 years in city government. His official explanation was that he wanted to spend more time with his family. Certainly the suburb that had become his passion and avocation had consumed his days and nights. In September 1938, his political career almost cost him his life when an enraged laid-off city employee shot at Cain and city manager Canfield at the conclusion of a council meeting; Cain was unhurt, although Canfield received superficial wounds. Perhaps after guiding the suburb's explosive growth, steering it through the perils of the Depression, directing its war-time enthusiasm, and playing a key role in county politics, Cain was simply tired.

But Cain also appeared to be losing his political grip. In 1934, the *Cleveland Plain Dealer* had described Cleveland Heights as "the prettiest little closed political corporation in the county." Council's public meetings, the writer charged, were meaningless rituals; all important business was done at private meetings, from which citizens and reporters were excluded. (Perhaps the closed meetings were a holdover from the period when the trustees met in the old voting booth at Mayfield and Superior.) This political strategy might have worked when Cain became mayor in 1914 and Cleveland Heights was a village of approximately 8,000 relatively homogeneous residents. The emergencies of the Depression and

WORLD WAR II MEMORIAL. The simple monument at the north end of Cumberland Park lists the names of the 5,400 Cleveland Heights residents who served their country in this war. (Cleveland Press Collection.)

then the war had probably strengthened Cain's hold on local government. In 1945, however, Cleveland Heights was a very different place: it had a population of about 56,000 of diverse class and religious backgrounds. Elected officials, including Cain, could no longer take for granted residents' unquestioning assent. And when the war-time crisis ended, public opposition to Cain emerged.

This opposition was expressed most vociferously by the *Heights Press*, which had endorsed Cain for years and remained Republican, but which turned increasingly against him and his colleagues on council. In 1944, the paper headlined repeated shortfalls in the city's water department, which the administration had covered by illegal transfers from the city's general fund. In January 1945, the paper reported the dumping of raw garbage into the Bluestone quarries. Editorials complained that Cain and council members kept their salaries a secret and accused Cain of taking an illegal salary raise. Echoing the *Plain Dealer*'s earlier accusation, the *Heights Press* charged Cain with creating a "dictatorship," which excluded the press and the public from important executive sessions of council and which paid Cain $6,000 a year, although he was seldom at city hall.[22] In May 1945, voters turned down a charter amendment that would have allowed the city council to raise the tax levy without going to the voters. This defeat provided the immediate impetus for Cain's decision not to run again.

Emboldened, a slate of opponents calling themselves the Better Government League of Cleveland Heights entered the November election. The slate included the first woman candidate for council, Mrs. W.A. DeOtt. The league's platform was markedly pro-growth, emphasizing better transportation and recreation, cooperation with local businesses, and "long-range planning." These candidates also urged that a community recreation center be built in Forest Hill Park across the street from the World War II Memorial. But Cleveland Heights voters chose continuity over change and soundly defeated the challengers. The men who had served with Cain for years and Karl J. Ertle, who ran on the incumbents' slate, were returned to office. "The machine has again triumphed," wailed the *Heights Press*. The paper took a parting shot at Cain, reporting that the impressive stone with a bronze tablet at the Lee Road entrance to Cain Park was financed by asking city employees to "contribute" one percent of their wages for two months.[23]

Longtime councilman William C. Dunlap was chosen mayor by his colleagues. His January 1946 inaugural address boasted of the city's low tax rate and lack of debt. However, Dunlap was frank in his assessment of the challenges the city now faced. The Depression and the war had taken a significant toll on the city's infrastructure despite federal public works projects. City equipment and buildings were obsolete; services had been curtailed. Home-building and buying had been dramatically slowed for a decade and a half, cutting into the city's tax revenues. Dunlap hoped to return to "prewar standards" and to foster better public transportation. But, he conceded, "Our financial outlook is none too bright," and he predicted that voters would soon have to vote again on a tax levy."[24]

City manager Canfield also resigned. He had served the city for 42 years. Although it had been increasingly critical of him, the *Heights Press* now gave him high marks for administrative ability and integrity.

Life in Cleveland Heights would never be the same. Residents and leaders had responded courageously and generously to economic catastrophe and military cataclysm. During hard times, they gave to those who had less; during war-time, they had united against a common enemy. The national emergencies had initially heightened, then transcended class distinctions, creating a sense of community among diverse residents. These years of Depression and war left visible public reminders, especially in Forest Hill, Cumberland, and Cain Parks. These emergencies also left less visible emotional scars: hard lessons about how quickly economic fortunes can change, tragic lessons about how loved ones can be lost. Cleveland Heights residents had also learned that the suburb was no refuge from the problems of the city or the world.

The resignation of Cain and Canfield, who for more than 30 very formative years had guided the city, suggested new departures. Cain had remained more insular than residents, more committed to political independence, or isolation, as in his rejection of joint relief efforts and regional government. More significantly, Cain remained committed to a primarily residential streetcar suburb of single-family homes. His political opponents envisioned something else: a suburb with more commerce and more public and private transportation. The *Heights Press* accused Cain of being planless. More accurately, Cain had stuck with his original plan. This plan seemed less viable in the post-war suburban world.

5. SUBURB AT A CROSSROADS
CONTROVERSY AND COMPROMISE, 1947–1970

Art critic and historian Eleanor Munro grew up in Ambler Heights. It was only a short walk down Cedar Glen to the Cleveland Museum of Art, where her father, Thomas Munro, was director of the Education Department. Years later she described the neighborhood's gradual decline in the post-war period. She and playmates "followed driveways lost in greenery up to the foot of abandoned mansions, built in a boom, then vacated . . . . [W]e came to wide boulevards and saw . . . the signs of the city: a water-purification plant [the Baldwin Filtration Plant], a veterans' hospital, a railroad trestle . . . I began to see [the neighborhood] for what it was, an enclave of decades-old homes now too close to the inner city to be entirely fashionable . . . while the newer money . . . was streaming farther east."[1] Other Cleveland Heights residents, and a new, post-Cain generation of elected officials, also knew the suburb was not what it used to be, but they had no clear vision of where Cleveland Heights should go. At this crucial juncture of the past and the future, two pressing problems emerged: what to do with the huge mansions that had originally identified Cleveland Heights as an affluent, exclusive suburb and how to adapt a streetcar suburb to the automobile age. Attempts to solve these problems generated heated controversies and partially successful compromises.

The post-war years were the heyday of American suburbanization. For the first time since the beginning of the Great Depression, Americans had money to spend and things to spend it on. They started, or enlarged, their families and moved out of cities and into suburbs with energy and optimism. Federal policies spurred this out-migration. The GI Bill helped returning veterans pay for suburban housing, and federal highways helped them get there. The Federal Housing Administration's lending policies advantaged homes in new communities and white over black borrowers, encouraging the homogeneity of the populations and the architecture of newer suburbs.

Cleveland Heights population also grew, peaking at 61,000 in 1960. Most residents remained comfortably middle-class and up. In 1954, 70 percent of Cleveland Heights residents owned their own homes; 23 percent were employed as professionals or technical workers; 21 percent as managers or proprietors. (Comparable figures for Shaker Heights were 69 percent; 24 percent; and 31 percent.)[2]

This population growth and prosperity occasioned a flurry of new public building that had been delayed by the Depression and the war. In 1955, the city opened Denison Park, named for longtime councilman Robert F. Denison. Its construction at Bluestone and Monticello, on the site of the old quarry that also served as the city dump, was a belated acknowledgment of this rapidly growing, still relatively isolated neighborhood. City Hall expanded east along Mayfield, replacing small shops and stores for needed office space.

The baby boom and continued in-migration also necessitated a second great wave of school building: Northwood, Millikin, and Belvoir (now Gearity) Schools and Wiley Junior High. Additions were made to Roxboro and Noble Schools, Roosevelt Junior High, and to the high school when a levy to build a new one failed in 1957. Cleveland Heights High School graduated bumper classes

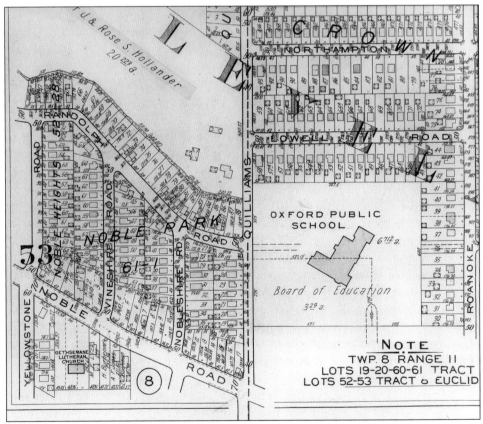

OXFORD SCHOOL NEIGHBORHOOD. *In 1941 the last large undeveloped tract in the northeast section of Cleveland Heights was on the verge of residential development. (Western Reserve Historical Society, Cleveland, Ohio.)*

each June: 534 in 1959, the second highest since 1942, and in 1965, 854 students, a school record. (There were also December graduations.)[3]

But Cleveland Heights, like the other older suburbs of Lakewood and East Cleveland, was growing less rapidly than newer suburbs to the south and east. From 1947 to 1952, Cleveland Heights population grew about eight percent, twice Cleveland's rate and more than four times East Cleveland's. Shaker Heights and University Heights, however, grew almost 25 percent; Lyndhurst and South Euclid populations almost doubled, as did Parma's.[4] The largest of the eastern suburbs and already densely settled, Cleveland Heights had little vacant land left. In 1947, the last new large residential development, and the first since the Depression, was initiated in the northeast section of the suburb off Quilliams Road. Within a decade, this development would become Runnymede, Mount Laurel, Brinkmore, Fenley, Stoneleigh, Langton, Burbridge, and Atherstone Roads. The Forest Hill allotment quickly became built up, not with the French Norman homes that John D. Rockefeller Jr. had first chosen, but with traditional colonials and new ranch homes. These were the choices also of new home-builders along Monticello Boulevard, which filled in during the 1950s and 1960s. (Monticello never got its streetcar; instead, it became a four-lane highway.) The days of the big allotments of single-family homes obviously were over. If the suburb's population was to continue to grow, residential development had to take other forms.

City council, then, had to figure out what forms new housing would take. The men who had sat on the Cain councils were gradually replaced in the post-war years. It had become customary (and in fact it still is) for an incumbent to resign before his term had expired so that council could appoint his replacement; this replacement would then become part of the incumbents' slate when he ran again. In 1947, newspaper reporter Jack Kennon successfully challenged that tradition by winning a seat without the incumbents' endorsement, perhaps the first person in the city's history to do so. By 1960, councilmen were a slightly more varied lot than they had been: two industrialists, William L. Ong of American Steel and Wire and John J. Dyer of Oglebay Norton; the journalist Kennon; lawyer Kenneth Nash; educator Merriam Clay Herrick, and advertising executive Fred P. Stashower. Like their constituents, these men—and they were all men until the appointment of Marjorie Wright in 1964—were firmly Republican and not wildly innovative. However, although they shared the conventional vision of a suburb as exclusive and exclusively residential, none had struggled to sustain this vision against great odds through the Depression and the war. Consequently, they were pragmatic enough to try to adapt it to the post-war situation and to try new strategies to maintain it.

The financial exigencies of the Depression and the shortage of manpower and building materials during the war had taken their toll on the city's housing stock and commercial areas. Council consequently became more willing to use public authority to control and maintain the quality of the city's buildings. In 1947, council established the Architectural Board of Review, composed of three architects, to oversee plans for all new buildings, and in 1948, passed a tighter zoning code. The functions of the 1921 Planning and Zoning Commission were divided between a Planning Commission and a Board of Zoning Appeals. Council's oversight of the suburb's development was then reinforced by these citizens. The city's own Planning Department, staffed by professionals, was established in 1961.

Council allowed new apartments to be built along Lee Road in the Rockefeller development and on Euclid Heights Boulevard at Coventry. Apartments in the original Euclid Heights allotment, however, showed visible signs of decay, and in the early 1950s, council declared war on "blight" and "slums" in this neighborhood. Their chief weapon was the purchase of parcels at Kenilworth and Overlook for a parking lot and a small park. Council also began to buy properties for a parking lot behind the Cedar-Lee shopping center. Except for a few disgruntled property owners, residents made little fuss about these actions even though they represented a departure from tradition.

The fate of the old mansions, on the other hand, generated acrimonious controversies for two decades, encouraging numerous lawsuits and dividing neighbors from neighbors and neighbors from councilmen. These homes symbolized the elite status of the suburb in its first decades. Many residents wanted to preserve that past.

The decline and re-use of the original mansions had begun in Euclid Heights and Ambler Heights. The original zoning code had permitted churches, schools, or philanthropic organizations to purchase and use a private home if it adjoined a park or streetcar tracks. This provision allowed the vast Howell Hinds mansion on "The Overlook" to be torn down in 1930 and replaced by the First Church of Christ Scientist. In 1939, the Warren Bicknell home on Harcourt Drive, very possibly the "abandoned mansion" visited by Eleanor Munro and her playmates, was sold to the Baptist Home of Northern Ohio. Council became alarmed and in 1940, tightened zoning restrictions so that homes could be adapted for use as institutions only if council decided that continued private ownership would constitute hardship. When Kenyon V. Painter's 28-acre estate at Lee and Fairmount went on the market in 1942, council refused to pay for extending the water and sewer lines, effectively blocking the property's residential development. Council did permit the Ursuline Sisters to purchase the estate for $37,000 in back taxes, and it became the site of Beaumont School.

The Depression had made the high taxes on these estates more difficult for owners to pay. The servants who had worked in the kitchens and cleaned the elegant living quarters had been lured away by better jobs in the war-time economy. And newer, more affluent suburbs farther from the city beckoned the very wealthy. Large homes such as the former estate of the murdered William Lowe Rice on Overlook Road (purchased by Frederick White) became illegal rooming houses in the post-war housing shortage.

In this rapidly changing context, council was compelled to make tough decisions. There were no clear guidelines. Euclid Avenue's "Millionaires' Row,"

WARREN BICKNELL MANSION. One of the great homes of Ambler Heights, this was sold in 1939 to the Baptist Home of Northern Ohio and is now part of Judson Retirement Center. (Cleveland Press Collection.)

FORMER RICE MANSION ON OVERLOOK, 1950. Purchased by Frederick White, this home was later demolished by Broadway Wrecking, as the sign indicates. Waldorf Towers now stands on this site. (Cleveland Press Collection.)

the model for Calhoun, had steadily deteriorated; most of these great mansions had been destroyed and replaced by commerce. This was not what Cleveland Heights officials wanted. Re-zoning for multi-family use seemed a viable compromise: a way to save the residential character of the suburb, if not the homes themselves.

Decisions made about the future of the Howard Eells estate at the intersection of Overlook and Euclid Heights Boulevard were predictive. The family had moved out in the late 1930s. In 1943, the Planning and Zoning Commission turned down the request of a Conservative Jewish congregation to lease the estate. Neighbors objected that there was already too much traffic from the Christian Science Church and Ursuline College, which had acquired the John Sherwin property across Overlook. In 1944, council decided to re-zone the Eells estate for apartments. In 1948, however, the Veterans' Administration proposed a hospital for the site. Supporters pointed out that there were few single-family homes in the neighborhood, much of which was already occupied by institutions, apartments, and the commercial buildings at Cedar and Fairmount. Nevertheless, the Veterans' Administration plan sparked lively opposition from residents and neighboring institutions, who as usual objected to traffic and parking problems. Some of this opposition may also have come from the operators of the new Doctors' Hospital in a converted apartment building nearby on Cedar Road or from the owners of another hospital planned, but never built, at Euclid Heights

EELLS ESTATE AT EUCLID HEIGHTS AND OVERLOOK, 1917. The fate of this mansion generated community controversy. (Case Western Reserve University Special Collections.)

OVERLOOK APARTMENTS, 1952. These apartments on the site of the Eells mansion maintained the residential quality of the neighborhood. (Cleveland Press Collection.)

and Mornington Lane. Former mayor Cain also opposed the veterans' hospital, appearing before council in a closed session. This appearance apparently turned the tide, for a once-divided council now voted against the proposed veterans' hospital. The site is now occupied by apartment buildings; the stone wall of the Eells' estate remains.

The Rice\White estate that extended from Overlook to Euclid Heights was also re-zoned for multi-family use, again over the protests of neighbors. The home was demolished, and in 1960 on its site were built the high-rise Waldorf Towers and facing Euclid Heights Boulevard, the Margaret Wagner Home of the Benjamin Rose Institute (now Concordia Care). Other Overlook residences were preserved by charitable organizations such as the Catherine Horstman Home for girls and the Cerebral Palsy Foundation. This re-use required only a special permit. By the mid-1960s, Case Institute of Technology (now Case Western Reserve University) had purchased for dormitories and fraternity houses several re-zoned properties off Overlook on Carlton Road at the very western edge of the suburb. Few private homes remained on Calhoun's "The Overlook."

The fate of Calhoun's own home on Derbyshire Road, deep within the Euclid Heights allotment, was somewhat different, but like the disposition of the Painter and Eells estates, it demonstrated the growing religious diversity of the suburb. The mansion's owner, the widow of Dr. George Crile, wished to sell the property.

CALHOUN/CRILE MANSION, 1944. The request by the Rabbinical College of Telshe to re-zone the property was vigorously opposed by neighbors. (Cleveland Press Collection.)

With her blessing, an Orthodox Jewish organization, the American Committee of the Rabbinical College of Telshe, asked the Planning and Zoning Commission in 1943 that the property be re-zoned for multi-family use, promising that the original mansion would be left intact. The organization's lawyer pointed out that Beaumont School and Ursuline College provided precedents for such re-use. Precedents did not impress neighbors, doubtless alarmed at the thought of sharing their Anglo-American enclave of Berkshire, Kenilworth, and Derbyshire with men wearing long beards and unusual clothes and speaking foreign languages. The commission rejected the college's plea. In 1954, the commission and council did approve the plans of the Hough Avenue Baptist Church to relocate to the site; it is now the home of the re-named Cedar Hill Baptist Church.

Council then tackled the problem of Cleveland Heights's most famous "rooming house," the estate of Dr. Charles Briggs. Designed by Charles Schweinfurth, architect for the very wealthy, the 30-room home had a ballroom and several outbuildings and occupied an entire block bounded by Coventry, Mornington Lane, Overlook, and Edgehill in the original Euclid Heights allotment. In its glory days, the estate had been photographed by Margaret Bourke-White and was the center of cultural and social events, including visits from neighborhood children like Betty Moore. When Briggs died in 1937, the

THE BRIGGS ESTATE. This was eventually re-zoned for condominiums; portions of the wall remain. (Cleveland Public Library.)

home was sold to Joseph Schermer, who rented out its many rooms and outbuildings and consequently ran afoul of the city's efforts to crack down on the "rooming house racket." In 1953, police verified that the estate was occupied by 19 persons, who paid almost $1,000 a month in rent. The city then moved to shut the rooming house down. Schermer fought back, first asking the city to re-zone and then challenging the constitutionality of the city ordinance against multi-family use of a single-family home. In 1955, an appeals judge backed the city, but the fate of the property remained in limbo for another decade. Although neighbors protested, city council finally permitted the property to be re-zoned for condominiums in 1964. Investors, including Charles Briggs's son John Briggs, bought the property, and despite threatened lawsuits, the original home was demolished and the new condominiums opened in 1965. The pool, ballroom, and portions of the estate's wall were preserved.

None of these changes had been easy. But compared to the difficulties occasioned by the Severance family mansions at Mayfield and Taylor, these earlier battles had been picnics. When John L. Severance died in 1936, he left a half-interest in his estate Longwood to Severance Millikin, the son of Dr. Benjamin and Julia Severance Millikin, and the other half of the estate to the Cleveland Museum of Art. (Millikin purchased this half in 1946.) In 1937, Millikin initiated plans to develop Longwood as a "high-class residential park" of 800 to 900 single-family homes on curving boulevards, perhaps in imitation of Rockefeller's Forest Hill.[5] A few homes were built on Crest and Severn Roads, but the rest of the development never materialized. In 1948, Millikin made a second effort to develop his property, this time as a shopping center. Led by Severn neighbors, the local chamber of commerce, and the Cleveland Heights League of Women Voters, citizens organized in opposition. Members of council, including Jack Kennon, who lived in nearby Forest Hill, also opposed the necessary re-zoning. It was defeated in 1950.

Less than three years later, however, Millikin made a third, successful effort to profit from his vast property. The time was riper. Other great mansions, the Eells and Rice\White properties, were in the process of redevelopment. Across the street from Longwood, Glen Allen, the home of Millikin's second cousin, Julia Severance Allen Prentiss, had been demolished in 1944, and a portion of it had been developed as single-family homes. (Neighbors insisted that these not be inexpensive homes.) To the west, Millikin's parents' home, Ben Brae, was demolished in 1953 after their deaths. More significantly, large shopping malls were being built in suburbs across the country. Nearby suburbs had also attracted

GLEN ALLEN. The home of Julia Severance Allen Prentiss was demolished in 1944. (Cleveland Press Collection.)

AERIAL VIEW OF MAYFIELD AND TAYLOR, 1949. The huge Severance estate would become Severance Town Center. Longwood is barely visible in the woods. (Bruce Young.)

new shopping centers: Cedar-Center in University Heights, the Van Aken Shopping Center in Shaker Heights, and Eastgate in Mayfield Heights. Clearly these were the wave of the shopping future.

Now Millikin threatened to sell Longwood for non-payment of taxes if council did not permit re-zoning for commercial use. He also donated 13 acres of the southeast section of the property for a school soon named after him, perhaps a public relations gesture. Mayor Henry Pirtle was sympathetic to Millikin's dilemma and in August 1953 introduced the ordinance to re-zone the property for commercial-park use. Council had already asked the Regional Planning Commission to make recommendations about the future use of the whole Mayfield-Taylor area. In March 1954, the commission recommended for a mixed commercial-residential use and against a regional shopping center on the grounds that it would damage existing business districts such as Cedar-Lee and would lower residential property values.[6] Pirtle explained to residents that the city needed the property taxes that a shopping center would generate; the alternative might be an increase in their own taxes. Disregarding this, neighbors re-grouped in opposition as the Cleveland Heights Home Owners Protective League. The league ran bold ads in the *Heights and Sun Press*: "DO YOU want a $25,000,000

95

commercial-retail trade office-apartment development in your backyard . . . DOES ANYONE seriously think that a project of this magnitude will leave the rest of Cleveland Heights untouched?" the ad asked rhetorically. And after council hired a zoning expert who gave the re-zoning his okay, the league responded: "YOU be the 'expert,' Mr. and Mrs. Cleveland Heights. The Severance Estate plans—are they ?? DREAM or NIGHTMARE??"[7] Pirtle forced the resignation of the head of the Planning Commission when she challenged the re-zoning. The League of Women Voters, the chamber of commerce, and the *Heights and Sun Press* re-joined the opposition. Opponents and supporters packed emotional public meetings. Council and Millikin hired still another expert, the Urban Land Institute, for still another opinion, this one also favorable. And in December 1954, council voted unanimously to re-zone the property with the provision that all plans for the property get the approval of council and a new board of control. Opponents were not finished, however. Sam Magid of the Home Owners Protective League filed an injunction that halted building plans until December 1957, when the Ohio Supreme Court upheld the validity of the re-zoning.

Millikin moved to the exclusive suburb of Gates Mills in 1960. After further amendments to the re-zoning legislation and other delays, Longwood was razed in 1961. All that remained of the elegant estate were the stables, deeded to the school district, and an inoperable marble fountain that sat abandoned for almost 40 years. In 1962, ground was broken for the regional shopping center, which was owned by Winmar Realty and named Severance Center to evoke the memory of the site's departed elite residents.

When it was completed in summer 1963, Severance Center was reputedly the third-largest enclosed mall in the country. Its official opening in September was attended by Cleveland's high society, the men in black ties and tuxedos. The mall was anchored by Cleveland's two most distinguished department stores, Higbees and Halle Brothers. Between them were dozens of specialty shops for the affluent

$25,000,000

and a smokescreen of fancy language around the MILLIKIN "Longwood" Estate

OPPOSITION TO SEVERANCE CENTER. The $25 million was the projected cost of the shopping center; the ad was placed by angry citizens. (Heights Sun Press.)

SEVERANCE CENTER, 1963. Anchored by prestigious department stores, the enclosed center was surrounded by 50 acres of parking. (Cleveland Press Collection.)

customers the mall hoped to attract. Encircled by a 50-acre parking lot, the center was designed not for those who rode the bus or walked but for those who drove.

Although neighbors had lost their long battle against the shopping center, city officials again compromised. To diminish the impact of this huge commercial intrusion into the surrounding residential landscape, the city mandated park land that separated the mall and parking lot from Taylor and Mayfield, and stands of trees that screened nearby homes.

The remaining portion of the Millikin-Prentiss property across the street was also re-zoned in 1954, again creating controversy. The Jewish Community Federation, the chief fund-raising and policy-making body for Jewish agencies and institutions, expressed interest in this location for a community center in 1955. The request for the necessary re-zoning was delayed by the dispute over the proposed shopping center and by the possibility that the eastern portion of the property would become the site of a second public high school. When the necessary bond issue failed in May 1957, Lutheran East High School got the Planning Commission's approval. The commission, however, turned down the Jewish Community Federation's request on the grounds that a community center would create too much traffic, "institutionalize" the neighborhood, and remove the property from the tax duplicate. In July 1958, as residents again packed city council chambers and hundreds more stood outside in the halls, council over-ruled the Planning Commission. The Jewish Community Center opened in 1960.

City officials had had no grand plan for the future, but with residents' blessings, or their opprobrium, council had simply adapted to situations as they arose. This same strategy, or lack of it, was employed as the suburb's primary means of transportation changed. Here there were even less clear guidelines to follow.

During the Depression and the war, Cleveland Heights residents had continued to rely on public streetcars and buses. In 1942, the City of Cleveland bought the Cleveland Railway Company and established the Cleveland Transit System (CTS), which continued service to Cleveland Heights. Especially during the war, when spare parts became difficult to obtain, the transit system's stock became dilapidated, and service was cut back. Residents, more dependent than ever on public transportation, were unhappy; so were elected officials, especially Mayor Cain. When the war ended, CTS promised improvements, including new express bus routes and the removal of the old streetcars and tracks. In 1949, the streetcars made their last Cleveland Heights runs. "Goodbye, Trolleys!" rejoiced the *Sun and Heights Press*.[8] With federal aid, CTS planned a new cross-town rapid transit system that would run from East Cleveland's Windermere Station to the Cleveland Union Terminal downtown. Although some residents now hoped that the old streetcar tracks would be used to extend the rapid transit into Cleveland Heights, this did not happen. Proposals in 1955 for a rapid transit spur up Cedar and Euclid Heights Boulevard to Coventry were justified as an effort to revive and rebuild the declining Coventry commercial district, but they went nowhere.

During Cain's last years in office, his critics claimed that he blocked new parking lots because he still saw the streetcar as the suburb's primary means of transportation: this was proof to them of Cain's inability to change with the times. With the streetcars now gone, the bus, and especially the automobile, reigned. Since the 1920s, of course, the automobile had spurred the suburb's growth. Its impact could be seen everywhere: the development of north-south streets, the appearance of gas stations, clogged main streets, and the continual need for street improvements. Postwar prosperity made car-buying even easier. The new colonials and ranch houses in Forest Hill and the northeastern section of town had attached garages that identified home-owners as having at least one car. Council responded to the resulting public parking problems by building the parking lots at Kenilworth and Overlook and behind the Cedar-Lee shopping center and by providing 50 acres of parking at Severance Center.

Meanwhile, the federal government's accommodation to the automobile set the stage for another Cleveland Heights drama. This continued for more than 15 years and ultimately united Cleveland Heights residents with neighbors in Shaker Heights, Cleveland, and other suburbs in a long, drawn-out battle against the State of Ohio and Cuyahoga County Engineer Albert Porter.

Plans for a federal highway system dated back to 1944, but not until 1956 and the passage of the Federal Highway Act did they receive adequate political support and funding. Cold War fears then legitimized spending money on highways that

STREETCAR AT COVENTRY AND EUCLID HEIGHTS. Streetcars were making their last runs in Cleveland Heights as the suburb made the difficult transition to automobiles. (Western Reserve Historical Society, Cleveland, Ohio.)

would efficiently transport military personnel and equipment in case of an attack by the Soviet Union. In early 1956, alarmed Cleveland Heights residents first got wind of plans for a federal highway that would run from Euclid Avenue through the Forest Hill development and east to South Euclid, Lyndhurst, and Highland Heights. They were reassured that this "Heights Freeway" was 25 years away.

In December 1963, however, Porter made public his proposals for the Clark Freeway (I-290), which would run east and west along the Shaker Lakes to I-271 in Pepper Pike with a north-south interchange at Lee. The *Sun Press* immediately reported that the eight-lane highway would eliminate 80 homes and 5 commercial properties in Shaker Heights.[9] Despite assurances that the freeway was in the distant future, Shaker Heights residents, led by Mayor Paul K. Jones mobilized immediately in opposition to what they interpreted as a reckless destruction of fine homes and priceless parkland. In response to this outcry by residents of an influential suburb as well as to a 1962 federal law requiring citizen input, the Seven County Transportation Land Use Study (SCOTS) was established in 1964 to assess Porter's proposal. At this stage, Shaker Heights officials and residents played the key roles in opposing this imminent freeway since it posed the most threat to their suburb.

Cleveland Heights officials followed Shaker's lead. In 1963, county engineer's maps showed that Cleveland Heights would be on the paths of *four* future freeways: the Heights Freeway through East Cleveland, Cleveland Heights, South

99

Euclid, and Lyndhurst; the Central Freeway along Cedar through the center of Cleveland Heights; and the north-south Lee Freeway, which would connect the proposed Clark Freeway to Interstate 90. The Clark Freeway also endangered Cleveland Heights since the western boundaries of the Shaker Lakes are in Cleveland Heights, and the freeway would take some homes on North Park Boulevard. In January and February 1964, Mayor Kenneth Nash pointed out that the freeways would carve Cleveland Heights into segments. The proposed elevated Lee Freeway, he said, would create "a Chinese wall dividing our suburb from the north to south." He promised to join forces with Shaker Heights against both the Clark and the Lee Freeways. Cleveland Heights residents organized and attended community forums such as one on "Blight and Freeways" in January 1965, at which future councilman Philmore Hart told the audience that the Clark and Lee Freeways would cost the suburb 1,000 homes. In summer 1965, Cleveland Heights city council passed a resolution against the Lee Freeway.[10]

In fall 1965, women's organizations proposed a nature center on the lower Shaker Lake that would serve the schools of both suburbs. The proposal allowed opponents to capitalize on the negative impact of freeways on the lakes and watersheds, thus avoiding what might otherwise have been interpreted as a rather crass battle over the destruction of expensive property in wealthy suburbs. Supporters of the nature center, including the mayors of both suburbs, hoped that it would block both the Clark and the Lee Freeways.

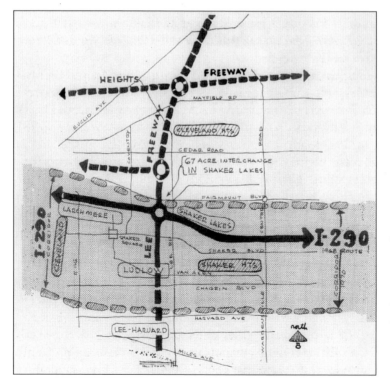

OPPOSITION TO FREEWAYS, 1970. Opponents drew this map of proposed freeways knifing through Shaker and Cleveland Heights. (Western Reserve Historical Society, Cleveland, Ohio.)

While SCOTS did its study for the next two years, the battle continued. In 1966, Shaker Heights and Cleveland Heights maintained their vigilance, both appointing transportation advisory committees. The state highway department also released a detailed panoramic picture of the intersection of the proposed Lee Freeway and the proposed Central Freeway that would have eliminated everything at the Cedar-Lee intersection except for the high school. Despite assurances from the state highway director that no final plans would be made until the SCOTS study was completed, Mayor Nash again blasted the proposal publicly. So did the school board and the Heights Chamber of Commerce. (The manager of Severance Center supported it.) In February 1967, Shaker mayor Jones assured an audience that Governor James Rhodes had promised that the Clark Freeway *would not* be built. Two weeks later, Porter assured an audience that the Clark Freeway *would* be built—Shaker Lakes or no Shaker Lakes. Rhodes himself, anxious to get the freeway route clarified before federal dollars disappeared, appointed a local task force to study the matter in hopes of reaching some agreement. Members included Richard S. Stoddart, chairman of the Cleveland Heights Mayor's Advisory Committee on Transportation. (Stoddart became councilman in June 1968, when Nash resigned to become judge of the Cleveland Heights Municipal Court. Fred P. Stashower replaced Nash as mayor.)

In summer 1968, a preliminary SCOTS report suggested a northern route for the Clark Freeway that would have touched only the northeast section of Cleveland Heights. This route spared the Shaker Lakes, but it angered officials and residents of Richmond Heights and Highland Heights. Cleveland Heights council initially adopted a wait-and-see position until the precise route was determined, but in June, council joined with the other affected suburbs to call for a moratorium on all freeway building.

Suburban opponents of the freeways were joined by Cleveland Mayor Carl B. Stokes. Cleveland had already experienced the destructive impact of highways that not only drained residents away from the city, but destroyed the neighborhoods in the highways' paths. Cleveland's population dropped from 914,808 in 1950 to 876,336 a decade later; freeways were one of the reasons.

In December 1969, Porter won a major victory when he persuaded the Northeast Ohio Area-wide Coordinating Committee (NOACA), which had succeeded SCOTS as a planning agency, to recommend for the freeway the southern route through Shaker Heights. Shaker Heights and Cleveland Heights immediately hired a law firm to help them block freeway plans and joined Cleveland in withholding dues from NOACA and condemning its decision. Residents formed still another committee, Citizens for Sane Transportation and Environmental Politics (CSTEP), headed by Cleveland Heights resident Worth Loomis. "STOP FREEWAY STUPIDITY," exclaimed CSTEP's advertising; "The Highwaymen are at it again! They want to make the Heights Area into an asphalt jungle. Once more we must stop these destroyers of our homes, parks, lakes, and neighborhoods."[11] A crowd of 2,000 citizens jammed CSTEP's public meeting in January 1970 to hear the proposal blasted by clergymen, state legislators, and members of the Stokes administration.

And suddenly it was all over. In February 1970, Rhodes at a breakfast meeting with suburban officials scrapped the plans for I-290 (both the Clark and the Lee Freeways). Rhodes was no particular friend of historic preservation or the environment; he had earlier proposed an alternate freeway route that would have eliminated most of the homes on Shaker Boulevard. But he was running for the United States Senate and certainly needed friends in these traditionally Republican suburbs. Rhodes lost his contest, but the suburbs had won theirs.

A key player in this battle was the editor and publisher of the weekly *Sun Press*, Harry Volk. A former reporter for the *Cleveland News* and a much-decorated veteran of World War II, Volk founded the *Shaker Sun* in 1946 and merged it with the *Heights Press* in 1948 to create the *Heights and Sun Press,* later the *Sun Press.* Volk generally sided with the forces for progress and development. He had little sympathy for the former mansions of the Cleveland Heights elite, referring to them once as "outmoded mausoleums."[12] But he instantly recognized the devastating impact of freeways, and from the time that Porter revealed his plans in 1963 to February 1970, Volk kept the issue alive and Heights citizens informed. Freeways were front-page headlines every week, and there was little pretense of journalistic objectivity when, for instance, the proposed freeway was described as a "concrete and steel monster." In spring 1964, *Sun Press* headlines prematurely shouted that, according to a reliable source, "CLARK FREEWAY IS DEAD ISSUE." When Rhodes finally killed the freeway, he revealed that he had been Volk's source and gave the editor much of the credit for the freeway's demise. Rhodes did not say why he allowed the battle to continue for another six years. Volk himself applauded the "angry, concerned citizens, acting with intelligence [who] make our democracy work. This is people power."[13] Volk was also a champion of racial integration and the preservation of the environment and an opponent of the war in Vietnam. The death of the Clark Freeway, however, was Volk's most successful crusade.

The battle against the freeways, like the Depression and the war, reminded residents that they were part of the larger, national picture: what happened in Washington, D.C., Columbus, and Cleveland had important implications for them. The battle also strengthened important political connections with other suburbs, especially Shaker Heights; these connections would pay off later as these older suburbs continued to be disadvantaged by federal policies. Cleveland Heights did not solve its transportation problems, however. It did not get a much-discussed rapid transit extension to Severance Center proposed by CTS in 1966 and supported by the mayor's advisory committee. And when I-271 was completed, it linked newer suburbs to the south and east directly to I-90 and downtown Cleveland, making them even more attractive to suburbanites.

Faced with unprecedented problems and contentious residents, Cleveland Heights officials compromised: they cautiously adapted to change and simultaneously tried to preserve the best of the suburb's past. Council allowed the demolition of some of the suburb's great homes—Eells, Rice\White, Calhoun, and the Severance families'—and allowed the re-use of others such as the

HARRY VOLK. The editor of the Sun Press *successfully fought the Clark and Lee Freeways. (Cleveland Press Collection.)*

Bicknell, Painter, and Briggs estates. These oldest mansions then became the locations of the suburb's most significant new buildings. Many great and gracious mansions remained, and if Cleveland Heights was no longer identified as the premier home of Cleveland's very elite, it had become home to handsome high-rise apartments and university dormitories, graciously housed charitable institutions, and a mall that initially aspired to elegance. The defeat of the freeways was a great victory for the community. It had preserved homes, lakes, parks, the residential character, and the social fabric of the community. The streetcar suburb's existing thoroughfares were also preserved. These were now used by buses and cars that continued to alter the residential and commercial landscapes. In another compromise, the city continued to widen streets and build parking lots, but the suburb's transition from streetcar to automobile was never completely successful.

In this post-war period, organized citizens emerged as a formidable political force. More firmly committed to the past than council, residents resisted change more vigorously—at least change in their own backyards. This citizen activism was a portent of the political ferment that would soon gather in strength but take a different direction. Harry Volk had complimented residents' "people power."

Volk himself and Fred P. Stashower, Cleveland Heights first Jewish mayor, also illustrated another powerful presence, the suburb's Jewish population. They too had changed the suburb.

103

6. Suburban Diaspora
Jews and Cleveland Heights, 1887–1970

In February 1924, at the ground-breaking for the new temple of B'nai Jeshurun congregation, Rabbi Abraham Nowak declared, "This marks the realization of an old cherished dream and the beginning of a new lease on life."[1] Nowak articulated the hopes of his congregation and the thousands of Jews who moved to Cleveland Heights. This move, first of the very elite and then of the middle class, constituted the first significant challenge to the suburb's ethnic and religious homogeneity and created tensions and difficulties for decades. Nevertheless, the diaspora which Nowak and his hopeful congregation represented ultimately turned this Anglo-American suburb into a lively, cosmopolitan, richly diverse community.

Other large American cities with significant Jewish populations, such as Boston, Chicago, Los Angeles, Washington, D.C., and New York, also experienced this exodus to the suburbs. As Jews pursued the amenities and upward social mobility of suburban life, their immigration patterns roughly paralleled those of non-Jews. Elite Jewish families, usually German, moved to the suburbs in the 1910s and 1920s. They were followed by the much larger out-migration of middle-class families, usually Eastern European, in the 1930s and after World War II. According to Judah Rubinstein and Sidney Z. Vincent, this migration from city to suburb took place "first, most dramatically, and most completely in Cleveland."[2]

The first Jews arrived in Cleveland in 1839 from Bavaria. They worked as peddlers, small shop-owners, and skilled artisans. Their success in Cleveland's prospering commercial economy attracted other Jews. In 1860, the city's 200 Jewish families constituted about 3.5 percent of its population. They settled first in the Woodland neighborhood from the Central Market to East 55th Street. Here they established the first significant Jewish social service agencies, the Jewish Orphan Asylum (now Bellefaire Jewish Children's Bureau) and the Montefiore Home for the elderly. This neighborhood was also home to the two largest Jewish congregations, Anshe Chesed and Tifereth Israel, which dominated the life of the Jewish community by virtue of their members' prosperity and social status. During the 1860s and 1870s, these congregations began to identify with the

American Reform tradition of Judaism as members sought assimilation into the dominant culture.

Beginning in the 1880s, German and Hungarian Jews were joined by an enormous second wave of immigrants from Eastern Europe, most of them Orthodox. From 1905 to 1912, an estimated 35,000 Jews arrived in Cleveland; between 1895 and 1920, at least 25 new Orthodox synagogues were established. These newcomers also moved first into the Woodland area, where they worked in skilled trades such as cigar-rolling or garment-making or as clerks in Jewish-owned shops. Alarmed and concerned by this huge influx of immigrants, established Cleveland Jewry encouraged their Americanization by founding the Council Educational Alliance, a Jewish settlement house. In 1920, Jews constituted an estimated 10 percent of Cleveland's population.[3]

At the turn of the twentieth century, the earliest Jewish arrivals had begun to move out of the Woodland neighborhood east and north into Glenville, once the site of the race track and golf club for Cleveland's elite and now a comfortable, middle-class urban neighborhood. In the 1920s, the second wave of immigrants also moved into Glenville as well as east and south into the Kinsman-Mount Pleasant neighborhood. Glenville replaced Woodland as the center of Jewish social, commercial, and religious life. East 105th Street was lined with Jewish bakeries, pharmacies, shops, and important charitable and religious institutions.

B'NAI JESHURUN. The first large Jewish congregation in Cleveland Heights broke ground for its Byzantine-inspired building in 1924. (Western Reserve Historical Society, Cleveland, Ohio.)

105

Mount Sinai Hospital opened there in 1916; the Jewish Orphan Home, the Orthodox alternative to the Jewish Orphan Asylum, in 1919; and the Jewish Orthodox Home for the Aged, in 1921. On Ansel Road, Tifereth Israel built The Temple with its magnificent dome in 1924. Anshe Emeth congregation in 1921 moved from East 37th Street into a vast new building on East 105th. This Cleveland Jewish Center included an auditorium, classrooms, gymnasium, and swimming pool for the growing community. Anshe Emeth soon joined the Conservative movement. Jewish students attended Cleveland public schools. Glenville High School acquired a predominantly Jewish student body and a reputation for academic excellence.

The two Reform congregations had already taken the first step toward suburban out-migration. Less than two decades after Lake View Cemetery opened, Jews also established a cemetery on the heights of East Cleveland Township. In 1887, Tifereth Israel purchased 20 acres just east of Lake View along Mayfield Road. In 1890, Tifereth Israel and Anshe Chesed formed the United Jewish Cemetery Association to maintain Mayfield Cemetery. Both congregations were still located in the Woodland neighborhood, but this cemetery, although smaller and less grand than Lake View, promised Jews a place in the suburbs sometime in their future. (Ironically, neither of these Reform congregations moved to Cleveland Heights.)

In 1905, members of the Jewish elite established in the new village of Cleveland Heights the Oakwood Club, a golf club that was their counterpart of Calhoun's

OAKWOOD CLUB, 1911. The exclusive golf club was the Jewish counterpart of Calhoun's Euclid Club. (Western Reserve Historical Society, Cleveland, Ohio.)

OAKWOOD CLUB LADIES ON THE LINKS. The club produced many fine women golfers. (Case Western Reserve University Special Collections and the Oakwood Club.)

LADIES ON THE LINKS

Betsy Eckhouse showing perfect form

Myra Printz, City Champion 1919 and 1923

Edna Hays, medalist, City Championship 1919

Jennie Joseph, runner up, City Championship 1912

Cora Joseph, 4th place, 1st City Championship 1910

Euclid Club. Its founders were bankers, successful merchants, and professionals. They were still city-dwellers but lived in Cleveland's affluent neighborhoods with other socially prominent Clevelanders. Bankers and street railway entrepreneurs, Leopold J. Wolf and Moses J. Mandelbaum, the two largest subscribers to the new club, lived near one another in the Wade Park/University Circle neighborhood. Subscribers Morris Black, a manufacturer of women's garments, and Salmon P. Halle, owner of a women's clothing store, lived on elegant Bolton Street (now East 86th Street).

In the next decade and a half, simultaneously with the *Cleveland Blue Book* families, these wealthy Jews (some also in the *Blue Book*) began their migration into Cleveland Heights. On the private drive that bordered Oakwood, its members built homes that rivaled those on Fairmount Boulevard. Here Isaac Joseph and Julius Feiss, owners of the Joseph and Feiss Company, a large clothing manufacturer, were joined by other club members. Affluent Jewish families also lived in Euclid Heights, Euclid Golf, and the Van Sweringen allotments. Baruch Mahler, owner of the Heights Center Building, lived on Harcourt Drive in Ambler Heights. So did Samuel H. Halle of Halle Brothers department store. Samuel H. Halle and his brother Salmon P., sons of early arrival Moses Halle, had purchased a hat and furrier shop in 1891, which by 1910 had moved to Euclid Avenue in the heart of the city's central business district. By the time Samuel H. Halle moved to Ambler Heights, Halle Brothers had become the city's most elegant department store. Salmon P. Halle lived on Oakwood Drive.

Sensitive to this movement, the *Jewish Review and Observer* began to advertise suburban homes and businesses for the Jewish elite. The Heights Savings and Loan announced its opening: "of Great Interest to those residing in the Heights." A realtor described a "brick house in perfect condition . . . finished ballroom on third . . . A bargain for quick sale—$30,000" in the Euclid Heights development.[4]

SAMUEL HALLE HOME, 1916. Built c. 1906 for Jerome Zerbe, this Georgian Revival residence in Ambler Heights is now the home of the president of Case Western Reserve University. (Case Western Reserve University Special Collections.)

Throughout the 1920s, this first wave of very wealthy Jews was joined by middle-class shopkeepers and professionals, who traveled from Glenville south on Superior Road to the Mayfield corridor between the cemetery and the Oakwood Club. In 1919, trustees Wolf and Mandelbaum had already persuaded the Montefiore Home to move just east of the cemetery. Boston architect Charles Greco designed the home's imposing Georgian revival brick structure in keeping with the suburb's Anglo-American architecture. In 1923, the first Jewish congregation entered Cleveland Heights. The Heights Orthodox Congregation worshiped in a Euclid Heights Boulevard home before buying a building on Superior near Mayfield. In 1937, the congregation changed its name to the Heights Jewish Center. Jewish merchants opened shops in the commercial district at Mayfield and Superior. The meat and grocery shops, barbers, tailors, beauty shops, and banks of Coventry Road catered to a Jewish clientele. By 1926, an estimated 5,000 Jews lived in Cleveland Heights.[5]

These Jews entered a community that emphatically defined itself not only as Anglo-American, but as Christian. During the 1920s, established and new congregations built large, imposing houses of worship. Like private homes, churches re-affirmed the suburb's affluence and reinforced the class differences between neighborhoods. The most elite congregations built along Fairmount Boulevard. The Episcopalians of St. Paul's moved from their Euclid Avenue location, merged with the congregation of St. Martin's, and in 1928 replaced its small chapel with a new structure at Fairmount and Coventry. Across the street, Fairmount Presbyterian Church constructed a large parish house. The Methodists who in 1904 had built the unassuming Gothic church on Hampshire and Superior moved to a monumental French Gothic Revival building on Lee Road and became Church of the Saviour. On Cedar Road, the growing congregation of St. Ann added a handsome Beaux Arts school building to its recreation hall and rectory in 1925, and Grace Lutheran completed its English Gothic Revival building in 1927. The major Protestant denominations had also built more modest structures in more modest neighborhoods. A second Methodist congregation built Church of the Cross on Caledonia Avenue in 1925. Lutherans built Messiah Lutheran at DeSota and Berkeley Avenues and Gethsemane Evangelical Lutheran Church (now Mount Olive Evangelical Lutheran Church) at Noble Road and Yellowstone Road. Presbyterians maintained Cleveland Heights Presbyterian at Mayfield and Preyer Road, Noble Road Presbyterian, and Heights United Presbyterian at Washington Boulevard and Lee Road. In 1927, the *Heights Press* boasted that Cleveland Heights was "the city of churches."[6]

The first sizeable in-migration of non-elite Jews into this "city of churches" in the 1920s did not always get a warm welcome. Individual Jews sometimes met prejudice. Jacob M. Lieberman moved to East Fairfax in 1922 and a half-century later remembered his early treatment. "When I came over here, they didn't like the idea of me moving here, and I'll tell you why. Because I'm Jewish, and there was nothing but a few Germans and Bohemians living here." Lieberman won over his neighbors, however, by giving them rides downtown: "Before long I had my car filled up with Bohemians and Germans."[7]

Although Lieberman recalled a happy ending to his story, the 1920s were also years when the United States Congress passed laws to restrict immigration from south and eastern Europe, the source of much Jewish immigration. The Klu Klux Klan, whose enemies now included Jews and Catholics as well as African Americans, achieved the height of its political power. Xenophobia, racism, and religious intolerance were not confined to congressmen or Klan members, however. In spring 1924, ten Cleveland Heights Protestant congregations instituted a program that allowed students to be excused from one hour of school a week to attend classes in religious education in nearby churches. The school board okayed the arrangement despite vigorous protests by Rabbi Abba Hillel Silver and Bishop Joseph Schrembs that the arrangement violated the separation of church and state. In fall 1924, Cleveland Heights residents thwarted the efforts of the Jewish Orphan Asylum to move to Quilliams Road. Their distrust of the Jewish institution outweighed the orphanage's promise to build a new public school on the site.

When B'nai Jeshurun•congregation first sought a new home in Cleveland Heights, it too encountered difficulties. Founded in 1866 by Hungarian Jews, B'nai Jeshurun replaced an Orthodox with a Conservative rabbi, Abraham Nowak, in 1923. After selling its building at East 55th and Scovill Avenue, the congregation bought two lots in the suburb. One in the Euclid Heights allotment was zoned only for single-family homes; the second was too small. The congregation then chose a location on Mayfield just east of Lee, where the February 1924 ground-breaking took place. "We are pioneers on the heights," said Nowak, forgetting the Oakwood Club and *Blue Book* Jews who had arrived earlier. "Let us build in the spirit . . . of fine fellowship . . . so that true brotherhood and not mere toleration may be established between Jews and non-Jews."[8] The rabbi and his congregation immediately discovered that his neighbors were not brotherly. The new temple was across the street from the Rockefeller development. Its residential properties would soon have racially restrictive deeds, and the prospect of a large Jewish institution across the street from the development's cornerstone commercial building dismayed the Rockefeller interests. They offered to exchange the temple's property for a much larger 16-acre site, half a mile away opposite the Forest Hill estate on the west side of Superior. The congregation actually halted construction for two months until negotiations for this alternate site fell through.

This beginning was inauspicious, but B'nai Jeshurun made efforts to please its new neighbors. It celebrated its sesquicentennial on July 4, 1926, with a raising of the American flag attended by Mayor Cain and other dignitaries: "the services will not be religious," pointed out the *Cleveland Heights Dispatch*.[9] When the temple opened in August 1926, the mayor and the pastors of Catholic and Protestant churches were present. The temple's sanctuary seated 2,000, and its auditorium, another 1,200. The building also contained a library, bowling alleys, a dining room, and a ballroom. Like Anshe Emeth's Jewish Center, this was intended to provide for all the needs of the growing Jewish community. Although the building's Byzantine-inspired architecture contrasted with the more traditional Montefiore Home across the street, B'nai Jeshurun congregation suburbanized its name and became the Temple on the Heights.

By 1930, the Jewish newcomers had already changed the suburb's ethnic composition. In 1920, that population had been overwhelmingly native born and Anglo American. Ten years later, however, more than 15 percent were foreign-born: the greatest numbers were from Germany, Russia, Czechoslovakia, and Hungary.[10]

These Cleveland Heights Jews shared the hard times of the Depression. Small numbers were given direct relief by the Jewish Social Service Bureau. Many more simply tightened their belts or hoped for work relief from the city or the federal government. Families like those of Hope and Stanley Adelstein took in boarders to get by. She remembered a young stranger knocking on the back door, looking for work and food. Stanley recalled neighbors on Washington Boulevard losing their homes when they could not make mortgage payments; in summer 1935, he was hired by the foreclosing bank to cut the lawns of the unoccupied houses.[11]

B'NAI JESHURUN CONGREGATION, 1941. At this patriotic service, the congregation was presented with a flag and flagpole. (Western Reserve Historical Society, Cleveland, Ohio.)

The Depression did not halt the swift outward migration of Jews from Cleveland. In 1937, Jews constituted approximately 29 percent of Cleveland Heights families. Their children constituted 31 percent of the Cleveland Heights school population; this compared with 6.6 percent of the school population in Cleveland, 7 percent in East Cleveland, and 18.5 percent in Shaker Heights. Jews were heavily concentrated in the apartments, duplexes, and single homes close to Jewish institutions along Mayfield east to Taylor, on Coventry, and on Taylor south of Mayfield.[12]

In 1940, there were three Jewish houses of worship in the suburb: the Temple on the Heights, the Heights Jewish Center, and Community Temple, a splinter group that Rabbi Nowak had led out of the Temple on the Heights. Cleveland Heights was the second largest Jewish neighborhood in the Cleveland area after Glenville. And the greatest suburban migration was soon to come.

As it did for other Americans, World War II created economic opportunities for Jews, elevating more recent European immigrants into the middle class. Cleveland Jews entered prestigious law firms, joined the boards of trustees of local universities, headed development firms, banks, and cultural institutions, bought sports teams, and were elected to Cleveland City Council and judicial positions.

CONFIRMATION CLASS, 1949. Led by Rabbi Armand Cohen, Park became one of the largest conservative synagogues in the United States. (Western Reserve Historical Society, Cleveland, Ohio.)

And for Jews, the war had special significance, for the American fight against Nazism contributed to a political and moral climate in which public expressions of anti-Semitism were less acceptable. These economic and ideological factors encouraged the escalating Jewish exodus into the eastern suburbs. And especially into Cleveland Heights, where there were already considerable numbers of Jews, important Jewish institutions, and moderately priced housing. Except in the Rockefeller development, there were no housing restrictions in Cleveland Heights, which was not the case in Shaker Heights and Pepper Pike. (All such housing restrictions were declared legally unenforceable by the U.S. Supreme Court in 1948, although they remained in effect longer by custom.) Historian Judah Rubinstein estimated that in 1944, 27,000 Jews lived in Cleveland Heights, an increase of 15,000 since 1937.[13] This estimate would make Jews almost one-half of the suburb's population.

Like their Cleveland Heights neighbors, Jews threw themselves behind the war effort. The Oakwood Club temporarily served as headquarters for a battalion of military police. Jewish men served as air raid wardens and like Alix Kates Shulman's father, on draft and ration boards. Their wives bought war bonds and organized block groups and scrap drives. Jewish names too appeared on the front pages of the *Heights Press* when men and women entered the armed services. Some did not return, including Sardou W. Abrahams of Blanche Road, Herbert L. Cohn of Washington Boulevard, Jerome Deutsch of Coventry Road, Phillip Eichorn of Superior Park Drive, Richard A. Fischel of Bainbridge Road, H. John Friedman of Edgehill Road, Sam Friedman of East Derbyshire Road, Manuel Lev of Washington Boulevard, Sanford Wasserman of Berkeley Road, and Jacob Lieberman's son, Earl, of East Fairfax Road.[14] On the World War II Memorial in Cumberland Park are listed the names of 6 other men named Cohn (and 17 named Cohen); 4 named Deutsch (Walter Deutsch also died); and 20 named Friedman (Sam Friedman also died).

During the war, two Jewish institutions had asked to re-use two old mansions, adding a religious dimension to this already complicated dilemma. Although allowing the Ursuline Sisters to establish Beaumont School on the Painter estate and Ursuline College on Overlook, the Planning and Zoning Commission in 1943 had turned down the request of the Community Temple to lease the Eells estate and the request of the Orthodox Rabbinical College of Telshe to re-zone the Calhoun/Crile mansion. Altering these Euclid Heights homes, symbols of the vanishing social elite, touched a sensitive community nerve.

However, in the war-time climate of patriotism and unity, there was gradual acceptance of new Jewish institutions, at least if they were built in already Jewish neighborhoods. This acceptance is illustrated in the eastward migration of congregation Anshe Emeth. By the time its Cleveland Jewish Center on East 105th was completed, members of the congregation had already begun to move out of the Glenville neighborhood. Anshe Emeth soon followed its members and in 1938, opened a small branch of the Center's school in the Masonic Temple annex at Mayfield and Lee and a year later, as these quarters were outgrown, a second branch in a home at Euclid Heights Boulevard and Cadwell Avenue. The congregation had first hoped to purchase the Painter estate, which was sold instead to the Ursulines. In 1942, however, Anshe Emeth purchased at auction the property of the bankrupt Park School on Mayfield, just east of the Temple on the Heights, and in 1943, opened Park Religious School, Park Day Camp, and Park Hebrew Academy in the existing school buildings. Through subterfuge, the congregation acquired more acreage on Mayfield from John D. Rockefeller Jr. In 1945, the congregation put the Cleveland Jewish Center up for sale and began plans to build a new structure on the Cleveland Heights site. In 1946, internationally known architect Eric Mendelson, a refugee from Nazi Germany, was hired to design the building. Two-hundred-fifty neighbors petitioned the Planning and Zoning Commission to reject the new structure. They objected to the terms "Cleveland" and "Center" being used to describe the suburban location, to a proposed outdoor theater, and "to more Jewish institutions crowding into Cleveland Heights," institutions that "outnumbered those of any other denomination."[15] The commission ignored the neighbors' protests, however, and approved the synagogue's request. Mendelson then created for the congregation the most dramatically modern building in the suburb and perhaps in all of Greater Cleveland. Families on nearby Whitethorn, Sycamore, Oak, and Compton Roads were a few minutes' walk to services and could admire the new synagogue's imposing dome, which shared the suburban skyline with the steeples and spires of its Christian neighbors.

Like B'nai Jeshurun, the congregation adapted its name and became Park Synagogue, one of the largest Conservative congregations in the United States. In 1952, Park played host to a conference of 500 Conservative rabbis of the Rabbinical Assembly of America.

The suburb was less accepting of Orthodox Jews. Reflecting both their own upward mobility and the war-time revival of Orthodoxy, growing numbers of Orthodox Jews migrated "suburban-ward." Their unconventional dress and their clustering in neighborhoods within walking distance of their *shules* made them highly visible and suspect to non-Jews and to more Americanized Conservative, Reform, or non-observant Jews. That suspicion at least in part accounts for the Planning and Zoning Commission's rejection of the Orthodox Rabbinical College's request to re-zone the Calhoun/Crile mansion. Two years later, the commission, at the request of some Jewish neighbors, turned down another Orthodox congregation that wanted to turn a Superior Road home into a Jewish day school.

In 1947, however, the commission permitted the Orthodox Anshe Marmoresh to build a new synagogue on Lancashire Road near Coventry, already a Jewish neighborhood. When the Orthodox congregation Oheb Zedek wished to move into Cleveland Heights, city officials stalled the building of its new synagogue on Taylor for two years. This large congregation, re-named Taylor Synagogue, resulted from the merger of several small Orthodox congregations that was engineered by the Jewish Community Federation. The federation wanted to avoid

PARK SYNAGOGUE. From the west, the synagogue's dramatic dome emerges from the trees.

the congregations' separate suburban arrivals and possible failures that would embarrass the Jewish community.

Despite this lukewarm reception, the Orthodox continued to arrive, and Cleveland Heights became the new center of communal life for Cleveland's Orthodox and Conservative Jews. Along Taylor, there developed a greater concentration of Jewish institutions than had existed in Glenville. In 1946, the Hebrew Academy, an Orthodox day school, built there. In the next decade, the Bureau of Jewish Education and Jewish Family Services also relocated to Taylor. After a legal skirmish over a newly required special use permit, so did a Jewish funeral home.

Jewish families moved into the new brick colonial homes on Severn, Shannon, Bendemeer, Berkeley, and Bainbridge, east of Taylor in the Severn allotment, and into duplexes on DeSota, Altamont, and Beechwood in Minor Heights across the street. From there, residents could walk to Davis Caterers, Unger's Bakery, Klotzman Kosher Meat Market, Moishe's Steak House, Goldweber's Food Market, Steiger's Kosher Market, Henry Weiss' Kosher Meat, Berky's Delicatessen, Goodman's Dress Shop, Max Goldsmith Meats, Isaac Kurson

HEBREW ACADEMY, 1953. The building of this school on Taylor Road signaled the growth of Cleveland Heights's Orthodox Jewish community. (Cleveland Press Collection.)

Kosher Meats, Honey's Bakery, or visit dentists Herman Adelstein or Edwin W. Horowitz or doctors Joseph M. Kaplan or Herman C. Weinberg. On Saturday, Taylor Road stores closed, and the street was lively with Jews walking to Sabbath services. (Well into the 1960s, Jewish delicatessen and bakery owners ran afoul of the suburb's law that required keeping a business closed on Saturday or Sunday.)

The new Jewish congregations—Park Synagogue, Taylor Road Synagogue, Anshe Marmaresher, and the Orthodox Shomre Shaboth on Taylor—participated in the enormous postwar building and re-building boom of religious structures. New churches reflected the new residential development in the suburb's northeastern neighborhoods: in the Forest Hill area, the Church of the Master on Monticello, Forest Hill Presbyterian (formerly Heights Presbyterian Church), and Hope Lutheran Church; Euclid Avenue Christian Church on Mayfield, Gracemount Gospel Chapel, and Kingdom Hall on Noble Road; Bethany Lutheran Church at Crest Road and Mayfield, and St. Louis on Taylor. Established congregations built additions: Community Temple, Noble Road Presbyterian, St. Paul's, Church of the Saviour, and Fairmount Presbyterian. St. Ann Church finally completed a massive new church in 1952; for two decades,

TAYLOR ROAD. The densely settled neighborhood of shops, offices, and institutions became the center of Jewish communal life. (Western Reserve Historical Society, Cleveland, Ohio.)

Reverend John Mary Powers had collected the building materials, including imposing stone pillars from a failed bank. Two newly arrived Jewish congregations adapted existing religious structures: "Gates of Hope" purchased the former home of Heights Presbyterian Church at Mayfield and Preyer in 1951, and the Beth Hamedrash Galicia congregation, Messiah Lutheran Church in 1953. The 1953–1954 *Cleveland City Directory* listed 15 institutions in Cleveland Heights under "Churches—Hebrew."

Harry Volk's *Sun Press* also acknowledged the growing Jewish presence in the suburb. Notices of services at temples and synagogues routinely appeared, sharing with non-Jewish congregations and institutions the "church news" section, which became the "church and temple" section in the early 1950s. Every December, the newspaper described Christmas and Chanukah services; every spring, Easter and Passover activities. Events of the Heights Hadassah groups were also news, such as the spring 1953 canvass for the Jewish Welfare Fund by 2,000 Jewish women from Cleveland, University, and Shaker Heights. The Park Synagogue's Couples Club's production, *Will Success Spoil Aaron Goldberg*, received several paragraphs on May 3, 1956. Jewish confirmation classes also made the paper: the Temple on the Heights confirmed a bumper crop of 155 persons in May 1954. Stories about Israel or travels to the new state were often reported, as were local marches celebrating Israel's independence.

The growing numbers of Jewish students changed the school calendar and enlivened its intellectual life. In June 1932, the date of the high school graduation was changed to accommodate the Jewish Confirmation day; the graduation speaker was Rabbi Barnett Brickner of the Euclid Avenue Temple. It became customary for rabbis to give the benediction or opening prayer at graduations. In the late 1930s, parents in elementary schools with predominantly Jewish enrollments, Coventry and Boulevard, successfully objected to their children's mandatory participation in Easter and Christmas programs and to penalties imposed when children missed school for Jewish holidays. Yom Kippur would become a public school holiday in Cleveland Heights. Jewish students brought to the high school their keen interest in liberal politics. In 1939, for instance, they led the school's Peace Council ("We, all of us, want peace. We feel, in a rather vague way, that something should be done about war") and the Student Discussion Club, which pondered "Communism, Labor problems, Youth problems, Democracy, and many other parallel issues."[16] Increasing sensitivity to religious diversity encouraged the Cleveland Heights school board to ban a religious census proposed by the Heights Ministerial Association in 1953.

The Jewish emphasis on education helped establish the suburb's tradition of academic excellence as it had in Glenville. Winners of the Women's Civic Club scholarships were often Jewish; one was Martha Wolfenstein, daughter of Simon Wolfenstein, director of the Jewish Orphan Asylum. In 1950, the school superintendent boasted that the high school students were among the brightest in the nation, based on their IQ scores. In 1951, one of every seven graduating seniors had won a place in the National Honor Society for academic achievement.

BOULEVARD SCHOOL, 1958. Dressed as farmers, these students planted trees on the school's campus. (Mimi Henry.)

The 1954 membership of the society included Phyllis Adelstine, James Amdur, Judith Bailin, Judith Ballanoff, Gloria Benovitz, Reva Bialosky, and Ina Cohen; there were almost no non-Jewish surnames. The high school in 1964 was ranked first in Ohio by the National Academy of Sciences, and in 1965, its 32 National Merit Scholarship semi-finalists ranked it seventh in the United States and second in Ohio. In 1969 and 1970, Cleveland Heights High produced more National Merit Scholarship winners than any high school in the state.[17]

This significant Jewish presence occasionally generated political controversy within the school district. In 1955, two candidates supporting the building of a second high school challenged incumbent members of the school board. The incumbents won, but a bond issue in support of a second high school was placed on the ballot in May 1957. The new school was to be located on Mayfield just east of Taylor, and its boundaries—roughly north of Superior and Washington—would include the most heavily Jewish neighborhoods. In unprecedented fashion, the Jewish Community Federation became involved. The federation protested vigorously that religion was not an issue. So did the school superintendent. Voters apparently didn't believe them and resoundingly turned down the bond issue. Neither Jews nor non-Jews apparently were willing to fund a new facility that might have been predominantly Jewish. Shortly thereafter, voters did approve a bond issue to build an addition to the old high school.

As their children entered the public schools, Jews had entered Cleveland Heights politics, as Fred P. Stashower's leadership of city council indicated. In March 1952, Stashower was appointed to council, its second Jewish member. In August 1947, David G. Skall had become the first Jew on council when he was appointed to fill a vacancy. A broker and member of the Oakwood Club, Skall lived on Fairmount Boulevard and belonged to the Euclid Avenue Temple (Anshe Chesed). He won re-election in November. Skall's election encouraged other Jews to run, and in 1949, there were two Jewish challengers: Sidney A. Eisenberg of Yorkshire Road and Leonard F. Auerbach of Revere Road. Neither won although both ran well in predominantly Jewish neighborhoods. When Skall resigned in December 1949, council appointed to his seat another Jew, Joseph Hartzmark, a member of the Oakwood Club and The Temple; he was re-elected in 1951. Jews were also elected to the Cleveland Heights–University Heights school board. The first Jewish member, Louis S. Belkin, served from 1947 to 1951; in 1950, he was board president. Others followed, like lawyer and long-time board member Norman E. Gutfeld.

Jews also participated in other important community institutions and rituals. The Jewish War Veterans' posts joined other veterans' organizations in the annual

YOUNG ISRAEL MARCH, 1970. A march on Taylor Road celebrated Israel's independence. (Western Reserve Historical Society, Cleveland, Ohio.)

Memorial Day parades and commemoration at the Cumberland Park War Memorial.

When the Jewish Community Federation looked for a site for a new community center, Cleveland Heights, especially near Taylor, was a logical choice. The proposed Jewish Community Center was the product of the merger of four institutions, including the Council Educational Alliance. The federation chose Glen Allen, the estate of Elizabeth Severance Allen Prentiss, because the federation estimated that 30,000 Jews lived within 2 miles of the property. The heated dispute between federation representatives, the Planning Commission, and neighbors was resolved only after city council over-ruled the commission and okayed the center. It was completed in 1960, the largest Jewish social service and recreation facility in the Cleveland area. Just to the north on Taylor, Council Gardens, a low-rent housing complex built under the auspices of the National Council of Jewish Women, opened in 1963. The new facilities reinforced the strong Jewish presence in that neighborhood and the suburb.

The Jews remaining in Cleveland were drawn to Cleveland Heights by these Jewish neighborhoods and institutions, especially as their own urban neighborhoods filled with African Americans in the postwar period. Novelist Jo Sinclair in 1955 described the mingled envy and social aspirations of the working-class Levines in *The Changelings*. For them, "the Heights" was "tea and poetry," the place where Jews such as themselves could own a butcher shop but could not afford to buy a house, the place to which more affluent Jews had fled. "The organizations have abandoned us—welfare, religion, the groups which give a Jew safety in his thoughts," worried Mr. Levine.[18] Jews like the Levines did not resist the lure of suburbia much longer. By 1960, almost its entire Jewish population had left Cleveland for the suburbs.

In 1961, an estimated 35 percent of the Jewish population of Cuyahoga County lived in Cleveland Heights. But the Jewish Community Center and Council Gardens would be the last significant Jewish institutions built there. The suburb's Jewish population was on the move again. To the east, University Heights and Beachwood already had large Jewish populations. The Heights Jewish Center had moved in 1948 to University Heights. After a lengthy court battle, Anshe Chesed had moved to Beachwood and dedicated Fairmount Temple in 1957. Tifereth Israel established a branch in Pepper Pike in 1969. The Temple on the Heights, the first large Jewish congregation up the hill into the Heights, had received a gift of property in Pepper Pike and voted to move there in 1969.

These Jews had been made uneasy by demographic changes, political turmoil, or signs of the suburb's diminishing exclusivity. Ironically, these were trends in which they themselves had participated. In seven decades, Jews had dramatically changed the suburb's ethnic composition even as they had altered the suburb's physical landscape with temples, synagogues, kosher meat markets, delicatessens, and Sabbath pedestrians. More significantly, Jewish residents had broadened the community's intellectual and religious horizons and enriched its political discourse. The street names and architecture of Cleveland Heights remained

Anglo-American, but its Jewish population had redefined the community's civic life.

The Jewish Community Federation, having just opened the new community center, was alarmed at the cost of re-locating or rebuilding in a more affluent suburb the significant cluster of Jewish institutions in Cleveland Heights: the Jewish Family Service Association, the Hebrew Academy, the Bureau of Jewish Education, the Montefiore Home, Park Synagogue, and Temple on the Heights as well as the several *shules* and the dozens of small businesses and shops that catered to a Jewish clientele. To halt the imminent exodus, the federation in 1969 established the Heights Area Project, which worked to establish better relationships between Jewish residents and city government and provided mortgage assistance for Jews wishing to move into Cleveland Heights. Jewish institutions pledged to remain in the neighborhood for "the foreseeable future." That future lasted barely another decade. The suburb's Jewish institutions and population continued to leave as another significant in-migration began.

DAVID BERGER MEMORIAL. The dramatic sculpture in front of the Jewish Community Center commemorates the murder of David Berger and ten other Jewish athletes at the 1972 Olympic Games. (Cleveland Press Collection.)

7. Changing People and Places
An Urban Suburb, 1965–2001

In 1997, Cleveland Heights leaders helped organize the First Suburbs Consortium with other "inner-ring urban suburbs." Like the first suburbs of the nineteenth century, these "urban suburbs" were close to Cleveland. Like the Cleveland of the late twentieth century, they had declining, less wealthy populations and aging housing stock and commercial districts. The consortium was a response to three decades of swift demographic, political, and economic changes. In Cleveland Heights, these changes generated public controversy, and in the case of race relations, shameful violence. As the century ended, residents who challenged, shaped, and accommodated to change had again redefined the suburb.

The most significant of these changes was the migration of African Americans into historically white suburbs across the United States. World War II had created for blacks the opportunities to earn good wages in war-related industries and to serve their country in the armed forces. Moving north out of a poverty-stricken, Jim Crow South raised expectations and made blacks a powerful political bloc in urban areas. These factors strengthened the civil rights movement, evidenced by the rising membership and militancy of the National Association for the Advancement of Colored People (NAACP). As it had for Jews, this war against a white-supremacist dictatorship helped create a political and moral climate more conducive to racial tolerance and equality. The civil rights movement won early significant legal victories against racial segregation in *Brown v. Board of Education* in 1954 and the successful bus boycott in Montgomery, Alabama, in 1955–1956.

Tens of thousands of African Americans had migrated to Cleveland in the 1940s, attracted by flourishing war-time industries. In 1950, Cleveland's 147,847 blacks constituted 16 percent of the city's population.[1] Despite the city's official gestures toward racial equity, including the establishment of a Community Relations Board in 1945 and a Fair Employment Practices law in 1946, *de facto* residential segregation persisted. Blacks lived almost exclusively on the city's East Side, moving first into the old Jewish neighborhood of Central/Woodland and then north and east into Hough and Glenville. Neglect during the Depression

A CHANGING PLACE. Three Monticello Middle School students shared a field trip to Denison Park. (Reaching Heights.)

and the war and the rapid influx of newcomers caused housing stock to deteriorate and city services to decline. In July 1966, a week-long race riot in the Hough neighborhood killed 4 people and injured 30 more. The National Guard had to be called in to establish order. In 1967, hopeful of quieting racial tensions, Clevelanders elected Carl B. Stokes their first black mayor. Although the city remained calm in the wake of Martin Luther King's assassination in April 1968, in July, a second serious race riot took place, this time in Glenville. The city's public schools remained targets of local civil rights organizations, which charged that the school board intentionally worsened the schools' racial segregation. In 1973, the NAACP filed suit against the Cleveland Board of Education; in 1976, a federal judge ruled that the Cleveland public schools must achieve racial integration.

Cleveland's population had already begun its steep decline as middle-class whites and blacks left deteriorating, racially tense city neighborhoods and schools in pursuit of suburban safety and comforts. African Americans moved first into the contiguous suburb of East Cleveland. In 1950, one percent of that suburb's population was black; in 1960, two percent. But homes in East Cleveland neighborhoods adjoining Cleveland began to change hands rapidly. White home-owners, made fearful by the block-busting tactics of both white and black realtors, fled the suburb. Its leaders made no effective efforts to halt the exodus or to solve the economic and social problems it created. East Cleveland rapidly re-segregated during the 1960s and 1970s. In 1980, its residents were 86.5 percent black. This re-segregation was accompanied by political and economic scandals; in 1988, the state of Ohio took control of the city's finances. In 1990, East Cleveland had the highest poverty rate of any suburb in Cuyahoga County.[2] This once-elite community about which Charles E. Bolton had boasted in 1901 had been completely transformed. Almost all that was left of the glory days when John D. Rockefeller was East Cleveland's wealthiest resident were its portion of Forest Hill Park and the elegant group of French Norman homes built by John D. Rockefeller Jr. For Cleveland Heights leaders and residents, the fate of East Cleveland taught a frightening lesson in how not to do things.

Cleveland Heights's own record on race relations was not a proud one. In 1930, one percent of the suburb's population was African American; most were

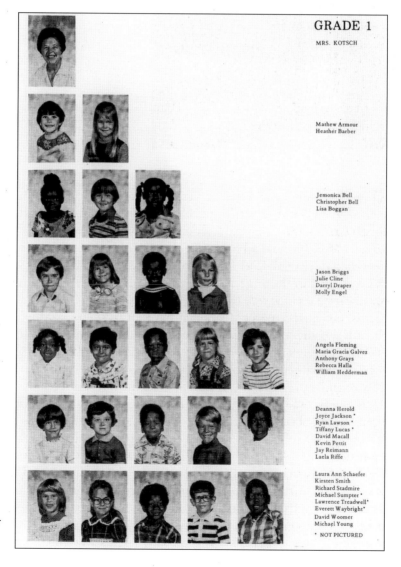

OXFORD SCHOOL, 1976. This first grade class reflected the racial integration of the suburb during the 1970s. (Cleveland Heights-University Heights Board of Education.)

GRADE 1

MRS. KOTSCH

Mathew Armour
Heather Barber

Jemonica Bell
Christopher Bell
Lisa Boggan

Jason Briggs
Julie Cline
Darryl Draper
Molly Engel

Angela Fleming
Maria Gracia Galvez
Anthony Grays
Rebecca Halla
William Hedderman

Deanna Herold
Joyce Jackson *
Ryan Lawson *
Tiffany Lucas *
David Macall
Kevin Pettit
Jay Reimann
Laela Riffe

Laura Ann Schaefer
Kirsten Smith
Richard Stadmire
Michael Sumpter *
Lawrence Treadwell*
Everett Waybright*
David Woomer
Michael Young

* NOT PICTURED

domestic servants. The properties in the Rockefeller development had racially restrictive covenants. When African-American entrepreneur Alonzo Wright moved into a home on Hampshire Road in the 1930s, it was bombed. Cleveland Heights's black population actually dropped from a 1930 high of 573 to 434 in 1950, a decline that probably reflected the demise of the great mansions and the departure of their servants. In 1960, the suburb's population was again one percent black; by 1970, two percent.[3]

Even these small numbers of black newcomers triggered racial violence. In May and June 1964, vandals smashed the windows of a Monticello Boulevard home purchased by a black family; police arrested six young men, two of them Cleveland Heights residents. Municipal Judge Bernard Ostrovsky found them guilty and denounced them as "night riders." In October 1965, two racially motivated bombings took place: one of the Euclid Heights Boulevard home of a black accountant, the other of an Edwards Court resident who rented property to a civil rights activist. In July 1966, a home on East Overlook Road was bombed, presumably because it was offered for sale on an open-occupancy basis. In May 1967, the same home, then owned by J. Newton Hill, the distinguished director of inter-racial Karamu House, was bombed again. The shooting of black folk singer Tedd Browne in July 1968 at the intersection of Cedar and South Overlook Roads was also racially inspired; his convicted killer had carved an "N" on his bullet for "the first nigger to come up Cedar Hill." In February 1969, the Taylor

RESISTING CHANGE. In 1967, this home on East Overlook, owned by J. Newton Hill, was bombed. (Cleveland Press Collection.)

Road office of black realtor Isaac Haggins was bombed. The *Sun Press* and several civic groups condemned the bombing. In September 1972, an arsonist set fire to the home of the Robert Appling family on Brinkmore Road. Mayor Oliver C. Schroeder Jr. described the arsonist as "afflicted with the most virulent of human diseases—hate and ignorance."[4]

Residents committed to racial equality acted, and energized by the on-going fight against the freeways, they moved more rapidly than elected officials. In 1964, concerned citizens, white and black, formed the Heights Citizens for Human Rights (HCHR). Already engaged in the civil rights movement in Cleveland, HCHR founders turned their attentions to their own suburb. The group's concerns and activities were far ranging. HCHR supported city council's stand against freeways but opposed proposals to redevelop by demolition the Coventry Road commercial district and to build luxury apartments in the Surrey Road area. The group urged stricter enforcement of the zoning code to halt the deterioration of housing stock. Along with the American Civil Liberties Union, HCHR protested what it considered an excessive use of force by police against a Students for a Democratic Society demonstration at a tennis match in September 1969. Most important, the group pursued fair housing. HCHR sponsored housing "checks" using black and white home-buyers and a "buy black" campaign to encourage African-American businesses. In 1969, the group won an Isaiah Award for Human Relations from the Cleveland chapter of the American Jewish Committee for its lecture series on "The Black Heritage." HCHR was politically active and visible. In 1966, members appeared before city council to ask for a fair housing law and in 1972, demanded that council pass equal opportunity employment legislation and that the city recruit black employees. In 1969 and 1971, HCHR endorsed challengers for city council posts.[5]

The on-going racial transition created frustration and tensions between whites and blacks. The St. Ann Church Social Action Committee in 1972 uncovered extensive racial steering by realtors who guided white families out of Cleveland Heights and Shaker Heights and black families in. Blacks encountered hostility and resistance. In a 1972 panel on their experiences "in white suburbia," black participants reminded the audience that racism persisted in Cleveland Heights. Dr. La Frances Rose, a sociologist at Case Western Reserve University, maintained that even small numbers of blacks made residents fearful of a black take-over. Another panelist, Robert P. Madison, was guardedly optimistic. He recalled that when he returned from his service in World War II, feeling "very American, very heroic fighting for democracy," he was initially refused admission to Western Reserve University's School of Architecture. When he built his home on North Park Boulevard in 1960, it was vandalized, and he received threatening phone calls. Madison wryly noted progress in the intervening dozen years: "One thing, we don't hear the bombs go off any more as blacks move in."[6] Madison later became chairman of the city's Planning Commission.

In 1972, residents formed another fair housing organization, the Heights Community Congress (HCC). HCC was rooted in Protestant, Catholic, and

HEIGHTS COMMUNITY CONGRESS, 1977. The goal of the congress, founded in 1972, remains a racially integrated community. (Cleveland Press Collection.)

Jewish congregations, and its first president was Reverend Charles A. Mayer of Hope Lutheran Church. HCC strategies were slightly less adversarial than those of HCHR, and its goal was as ambitious but more narrowly focused: creating and maintaining a racially integrated community without re-segregation. HCC's large membership included individuals and representatives of business, civic, religious, and neighborhood groups, city government, and the school and library boards. The organization hired a paid executive director, Harry Fagan, and rented an office on Lee Road. The Open Housing Task Force of HCC continued the work of the St. Ann committee, and monitoring the real estate industry became a primary goal of HCC. In 1974, HCC joined in a successful class action lawsuit against Rosenblatt Realty for racial steering. Like HCHR, HCC promoted maintenance of the suburb's housing stock, stressing housing inspection and sponsoring home improvement workshops and the Community Improvement Awards. To showcase the suburb's fine homes, as well as raise funds for itself, HCC initiated the Heights Heritage home tours. Its primary concern remained open housing, but HCC also assisted in neighborhood organizing and community outreach programs on human relations. In 1976, HCC won an Isaiah Award for Human Relations.

City council initially responded cautiously to racial change despite the continued racial tensions. When HCHR in 1966 had asked for a local fair housing law (the State of Ohio had already passed one), council demurred on the grounds that such a law would be divisive: "Conciliation and mediation, not legislation and enforcement, are the current methods required to heal the racial rift."[7] In 1967, when council adopted a law forbidding for-sale signs, a measure intended to discourage block-busting, East Cleveland, University Heights, and Shaker Heights already had such laws. In 1968, city council took other moderate steps, urging residents to form block associations to smooth the path to racial integration and in August, opening a realty clearing house at city hall to stabilize integrating neighborhoods and act as mediator between realtors and buyers. In summer 1971, the Bendemeer and Caledonia Neighborhood Associations complained to the Ohio Civil Rights Commission that realtors, including Isaac Haggins, made harassing phone calls urging them to sell their homes. Council then imposed a temporary ban on mass telephone solicitation in spring 1972 despite vigorous opposition from realtors. In fall 1972, after the St. Ann housing audit had been made public, council began a series of unsuccessful efforts to get voluntary compliance to fair housing standards from the real estate industry.

Activists, political challengers, and events, however, finally forced council's hand. In 1969, a slate backed by the Citizens Committee for Effective Heights Government criticized the incumbents' caution, describing them as "self-perpetuating and complacent." As if to confirm these criticisms, the victorious incumbents, Oliver C. Schroeder Jr., James C. Sennett, Fred P. Stashower, Richard S. Stoddart, and Marjorie B. Wright, described themselves as "experienced, non-political councilmen [who] have given us good municipal service AT LOWEST POSSIBLE COST!"[8] In 1971, challengers Lucille Huston and John Boyle, HCHR board members backed by the Citizens Committee, did win election; they were the first candidates since Jack Kennon in 1947 to break into the ranks of the incumbents. Two years later, the Citizens Committee backed two more successful candidates, Libby Resnick and Richard Weigand. The *Sun Press* called this upset "the end of the era of the self-perpetuating council." The ascendancy of a liberal majority on council was short-lived, however. Both Boyle and Huston were defeated in 1975.[9]

Then, after the efforts to achieve voluntary compliance from the real estate industry had failed, council finally took a more coercive approach. At its March 15, 1976 meeting, council passed a resolution that committed the city to "a renewed and expanded comprehensive program to promote the City of Cleveland Heights as a well-maintained, full-service residential community [and] to prevent racial re-segregation." Some residents present applauded the resolution, presenting to council evidence of continued unwelcome telephone solicitation by realtors, including Haggins. A lawyer for the Association of Black Realtists, however, argued that banning telephone solicitation would discriminate against them and threatened a lawsuit.[10] Council nevertheless passed legislation prohibiting block-busting, racial steering, and mass real estate solicitation. The legislation also established a housing board to investigate allegations of those tactics, a committee to examine the lending policies of local banks, and a preferred realty agent program that required completion of training in fair housing practices. Council also moved the city-funded HCC Housing Service to City Hall, along with some HCC staff; the service's first supervisor was HCHR member Barbara Roderick. The service showed properties to potential home-buyers, black and white. In November 1979, council described the goal of the Housing Service as "maintaining the rich cultural and racial diversity" of the suburb and acknowledged that this would entail encouraging "white home-seekers of all ages" to move to the suburb.[11] The city in 1979 joined HCC in a successful lawsuit against Hilltop Realty (now Realty One) for racial steering. In 1980, Cleveland Heights itself became the defendant in a suit financed by realtors' associations that charged that the city's housing programs discriminated against blacks; this suit dragged on until 1986, when the plaintiff withdrew from the lawsuit. In 1987, the city initiated the Heights Fund, which provided loans to home-buyers in neighborhoods needing racial balance; most loan recipients were white.

In 1976 and 1978, Cleveland Heights won All America City Awards for its efforts to maintain racial integration and religious tolerance. City surveys during the 1980s indicated residents' strong support for living in a racially integrated community. The city continued to support, with federal community development block grant funds, the open housing activities of HCC, the Cuyahoga Plan, another fair housing organization, and the city's own Housing Service.

Blacks continued to move in. The suburb's reputation for racial openness, its fine schools, parks, shopping districts, and modestly priced housing outweighed the possibility of racial hostility. Like Jews, African Americans dramatically altered the homogeneous suburban population. In 1980, it was 25 percent black; in 1990, 37 percent, an increase of almost 50 percent. All neighborhoods in the city were racially integrated although African Americans tended to be most concentrated in the northern sections of town, closest to East Cleveland, where housing prices were lower. Other east-side suburbs also gained black populations. In 1990, the Shaker Heights population was 31 percent black, an increase of 26 percent; the University Heights population, 16 percent, an increase of almost 70 percent.[12]

As blacks moved in, some whites moved out. Particularly noticeable was the continuing exodus of Jewish institutions and residents despite the efforts of the Heights Area Project. The Temple on the Heights moved to Pepper Pike in 1980; in 1986, Park Synagogue established a branch there, as did the Jewish Community Center. In 1991, the Montefiore Home moved to Beachwood. In 1994, the Oakwood Club made plans to move eastward and sell its property to Wal-Mart. The plans fell through, mostly because the far eastern suburb rejected the club. Cleveland Heights residents also objected to the further loss of green space to a giant commercial complex, storming city hall with petitions bearing 6,000 signatures. In 1987, Jews constituted an estimated 13.5 percent of the Cleveland Heights population. An estimated 7,000 Jews remained in the suburb, fewer than in the much smaller suburbs of Shaker Heights, University Heights, and Beachwood. Cleveland Heights still had the highest percentage of Orthodox Jews. In 1996, the estimated number of Jews in the suburb had risen to 8,600, an increase due in part to an influx of Jews from the former Soviet Union sponsored by the Jewish Community Federation.[13]

But the Cleveland Heights population had begun to decline. From its 1960 high of 61,813, it fell to 54,052 in 1990, approximately what it had been in 1940. This represented a 12.5 percent decrease.

Cleveland Heights residents were also less wealthy. Cleveland was hit hard by the de-industrialization of the national economy. Much heavy industry, the backbone of the urban economy since the Civil War, down-sized or moved elsewhere. Cleveland suburbs felt the impact. In 1981, the Heights Interfaith Council, established in 1975 by churches and synagogues, opened a hunger center at the Euclid Avenue Christian Church on Mayfield Road. The suburb's poverty rate rose from 5.4 percent in 1970 to 11.4 percent in 1991, far below the rates of Cleveland and East Cleveland but higher than the rates of other suburbs.[14]

These demographic shifts had enormous impact on the suburb, first and most obviously on the public schools. The number of students dwindled from a high of 13,254 in 1966 to 11,614 in 1972.[15] In that year, voters approved a bond issue to replace some aging elementary schools. By the end of the decade, the impressive 1920s colonial revival buildings of Boulevard, Taylor, Coventry, and Fairfax Schools had been replaced by smaller one-story structures. Intended to blend into the landscape rather than establish an imposing presence, the new schools also featured the open classrooms then in academic fashion. Roosevelt Junior High School was also demolished, and its students transferred to Monticello, Roxboro, or Wiley Junior High Schools.

ROOSEVELT JUNIOR HIGH, 1949. The ninth grade class posed in front of this handsome building, later demolished. (Cleveland Heights-University Heights Board of Education.)

The proportion of black to white students rose as white parents chose to send their children to the several nearby private and parochial schools, Catholic, Protestant, and Jewish. School changes became linked with the issue of race.

Like the city council, the school board worked hard to maintain racial balance within the district, especially in light of the suit brought by the NAACP against the Cleveland Board of Education. The schools, however, reflected the suburb's residential patterns. In 1976, three elementary schools in the city's northern section, Boulevard, Taylor, and Millikin, had enrollments that were 50 percent or more black. As the result of a citizens' committee recommendations, Millikin was closed in 1979, and its students bussed elsewhere. Millikin became a pre-school and day-care center. Boulevard and Belvoir (now Gearity) became magnet schools to achieve voluntary integration. Dwindling enrollments and the desire for racial balance also closed Northwood and the new Taylor School in 1984. Parents unsuccessfully sued to halt the closings.

Racial balance continued to elude the school system. Taylor re-opened as Taylor Academy in 1987 for students with academic difficulties. The NAACP protested because most of the students were black, but the school remained open. Taylor Academy became a political issue in the 1989 school board election; those who advocated its closing lost. In 2000–2001, the school district's enrollment of 7,094 was 22 percent white; 71.9 African American; 1.7 percent Asian; and 3.3 percent multi-racial.[16]

RAZING OF TAYLOR ROAD SCHOOL. *Part of the effort to replace the aging elementary schools, Taylor was demolished in 1974. (Cleveland Public Library.)*

The difficulties of racial transition were heightened by the political climate. During the 1960s, Cleveland Heights students, like young people (and their parents) across the country, had become political activists, supporting the civil rights movement and opposing the war in Vietnam. In the late 1960s, students at the high school organized a mass walkout when the school officials broke up a protest against the raising of the American flag. The high school administration then accommodated student unrest by relaxing the dress code and discipline but banned the Student Mobilization Committee, an anti-war group. Although upholding the ban, in June 1970 (a month after the shooting of students at Kent State University) the school board encouraged the students' right to peaceful dissent. The activism of black students and parents in the 1970s built upon this recent tradition of protest as well as the emerging tradition of black separatism and black pride.

As had Jewish students earlier, black students altered the school calendar and curriculum. In 1974, the Committee to Improve Community Relations (CICR), a group of black parents, and black students protested at the school administration building and school board meetings. Pointing to the fact that the school district observed the Jewish holiday of Yom Kippur, protesters demanded a holiday that would celebrate black history and achievements. The next year, the district observed Black Recognition Day on Martin Luther King's birthday, and the school board also agreed to hire more black staff and faculty and to add black studies courses to the curriculum. CICR member Bernice Lott was appointed to the school board; other African Americans soon followed. The high school added the Gospel Choir to its several excellent vocal and instrumental groups in 1975. In 1980, black students served on the high school's student council and had formed their own organizations, including the Brothers and the Sisters. The Gospel Choir was 50 strong; the Shalom Club for students interested in Hebrew culture had only 6 members.

Racial tensions also revealed themselves most dramatically at the high school. Fights between black and white students broke out in and outside the high school in January 1972. A series of fights in the halls sent students and policemen to the hospital in January 1975; black students alleged racist discipline. In 1976, the district hired a policeman to patrol the halls. In April, a scuffle between a black student and a white student escalated into fighting so uncontrolled and widespread that the school had be to shut down. Conflict between black gangs exacerbated the disorder, spreading violence out into the suburban streets. In February 1990, students were disciplined for gang-related fighting on Taylor Road. Gang rivalry culminated in the murder of a 14-year-old boy on Taylor on March 4, 1990.

Labor difficulties also plagued the school system; teacher salaries were a key issue. In January 1980 after 11 months of fruitless negotiations, the Cleveland Heights Teachers Union Local 795 of the American Federation of Teachers struck for two days. In January 1983, teachers again took to the picket lines; this strike lasted eight days. In November 1985, the teachers authorized a strike but reached a settlement in January 1986. Three years later, another strike was postponed, then averted in April at the 11th hour. Teachers voted to strike in 1997 but reached an agreement with the school board.

These unhappy events—racial unrest, labor turmoil, the closing of old schools, and the transfer of students to new ones—combined with national anti-tax sentiment to make residents less willing to support their schools. Voters turned down levies in March 1980, November 1987, May 1991, November 1991, March 1996, and November 1999. They also defeated decisively in May 1990 an income tax that would have provided school funding. The school board had to return again and again to the voters to keep the district out of the red.

Although students' scores on state proficiency tests placed the district on "academic watch" in 1999, the district demonstrated "continuous improvement" in 2000–2001. Students at all levels scored better than the national average on the California Achievement Tests. The high school continued to graduate National Merit semi-finalists (8 semifinalists and 6 commended in the class of 2001).[17]

Parents and concerned citizens stepped into the breach and formed grassroots groups like Reaching Heights and Coventry PEACE (People Enhancing a Child's Environment). These provided volunteer services, guidance, funding, and moral support to the school district in these difficult times.

Demographic changes, again reinforced by political trends, also re-shaped commercial districts. The importance of the Coventry neighborhood as a primarily Jewish shopping area had gradually been assumed by Taylor Road. The mid-1950s plans to renew Coventry by demolishing it came to nothing, and in the 1960s, the slightly scruffy shopping area re-emerged as home to the local counter-culture, the Cleveland Heights version of San Francisco's Haight-Asbury. A

COVENTRY PEACE. *Parents and children built the spectacular playground at Coventry Elementary School. (Coventry PEACE.)*

COVENTRY FIRE, 1991. The neighborhood rebuilt after this fire, its third in a dozen years. (Cleveland Public Library.)

harbinger of this re-invention was the arrest in November 1959 of Nico Jacobellis, owner of the Heights Art Theater (the suburb's first movie theater) for his showing of the allegedly obscene *Les Amants* (*The Lovers*); in 1964 the U.S. Supreme Court overturned his conviction, striking a blow for artistic freedom. Although the *Sun Press* called Coventry's co-mingling of kosher meat market, bagels, and hippies a "love-in," the scene was not always peaceful. In 1969, for instance, police battled a Hell's Angels motorcycle gang there. In the mid-70s, Coventry merchants sold antiques, water beds, health foods, jewelry, leather goods, and second-hand records, as well as kosher poultry. The neighborhood maintained its counter-culture image with summer street fairs that attracted thousands of people. Featured attractions included music, food, art, sidewalk stalls, and theatrically dressed neighborhood residents. Coventry's small shops and hippie aura, enhanced by the avant garde Dobama Theater and an alternative weekly, the *Free Times,* survived three costly fires from 1979 to 1991, the demolition of counter-cultural Rock Court homes for a parking lot, and a huge, concrete-reinforced, public parking garage completed in 1994.

Severance Center aged less gracefully, but like the Coventry neighborhood, responded to the suburb's changing population as well as to national trends. After it opened in 1963, mall owner Winmar Realty encouraged residents to think of it as a civic center, hosting art shows, public health immunizations, and other community events. The mall attracted not only the affluent suburbanites for whom it was intended, however, but others who were less welcome. In December

THE SPIRIT OF COVENTRY. Protesters in front of the Coventry Library demonstrate the freedom of expression that characterizes this neighborhood. (Roy Woda.)

1969, members of the radical Weathermen smashed windows and frightened Christmas shoppers. The mall also drew black customers; it was the closest shopping center to the black neighborhoods in Cleveland, East Cleveland, and Cleveland Heights.

Mall business suffered from competition with newer malls, especially up-scale Beachwood Place. In 1981, mall owners added a new wing and more stores. A year later, however, one of the original anchors, Halle's, pulled out. So did a prestigious men's clothing store, leaving 200,000 square feet vacant. Shoppers worried about crime, especially car theft. Security was tightened, and teenagers' access to the mall slightly restricted. In 1984, Winmar initiated a multi-million dollar renovation and expansion, and in 1985, six new movie theaters joined the mall, now grown to 100 stores and 987,000 square feet. But a discount store, Gold Circle, initially excluded from the center, closed after only four years. Other retailers came and went. In 1986, Cleveland Heights City Hall, including the court, police station, and jail, relocated to the periphery of the property in an effort to boost the shopping center's revival. The complex of municipal buildings and private commercial structures was renamed Severance Town Center.

Having taken its toll on nearby small shops and grocery stores, the mall continued to experience serious economic difficulties, worsened by the increasing dominance of retail markets by huge national chains. In 1988, Dillard Department Stores bought both Higbee's and Horne's. Horne's occupied the site left vacant

SEVERANCE CENTER, 1976. In its prosperous days, the enclosed mall became a community gathering place. (Cleveland Press Collection.)

by Halle's, so that Dillard now operated both anchor positions. In March 1995, Dillard pulled out, leaving the two anchors vacant. In that same month, an enraged former employee on a rampage was shot to death by a security guard in the mall's food court in front of horrified customers. As tenants and shoppers left, Winmar decided to replace the large enclosed shopping center with a much scaled-down, two-sided strip mall. Wal-Mart, Home Depot, Borders, and other national chains built giant "big box" stores. In December 2001, the shopping center was purchased by an investment firm, whose chief partner was African-American athlete and entrepreneur Magic Johnson.

As they had earlier, houses of worship reflected the changing community. Black newcomers to Cleveland Heights did not build new religious structures, as had early Jewish congregations. Instead, African Americans joined Protestant and Catholic churches or adapted older churches. Two of these adaptations had special historical significance. When the Temple on the Heights moved in 1980, its building, renamed The Civic, became the home of the New Spirit Revival Center. In 1982, the suburb's oldest sacred structure, built in 1904 for the Cleveland Heights Methodist Episcopal Church, became Christ Our Redeemer African Methodist Episcopal Church.

City council also changed. In 1965, all council members except Marjorie Wright were male; all were white; all were Republican. The victories and near-victories of challengers in the late 1960s and early 1970s, however, foreshadowed

137

CHRIST OUR REDEEMER A.M.E. The congregation purchased the former home of Cleveland Heights Methodist Episcopal Church (now Church of the Saviour) in 1982.

ST. ANN'S FIRST COMMUNION DAY. African Americans joined Cleveland Heights churches. (Karen Laborde.)

the growing liberalization of council. In 1983, Barbara Boyd became council's first black member. Boyd had the endorsement of the Cleveland Heights Democratic organization. Her election, like that of David G. Skall in 1947, signaled Cleveland Heights voters' acceptance of the suburb's newest arrivals. In 1999, council members Bonita W. Caplan, Nancy J. Dietrich, Phyllis L. Evans, Jimmy Hicks Jr., Edward J. Kelley, Kenneth Montlack, and Dennis R. Wilcox mirrored their constituency: three were women; two were African American.

Taking its cue from citizens, city council and city government played an increasingly activist role, trying to guide and direct rather than simply react to change. Simultaneously with its fair housing legislation, council had stepped up efforts to maintain the quality of the city's housing stock and commercial areas, much of which was 50 years old. It was crucial that racial integration not be accompanied by the deterioration of property and the decline of property values. Unlike racial issues, the preservation of property was a familiar, relatively uncontroversial responsibility that had begun with the zoning code and accelerated in the post-war fight against "blight." Council mandated point-of-sale and other systematic housing inspections. Federal community development block grant funds became crucial resources. In 2001, the city allocated more of these funds to housing preservation, including multi-family housing, than to any other eligible program or service. Three agencies that provided financial and other assistance to low-moderate income families and seniors for housing repairs—the Home Repair Resource Center (formerly Forest Hill Housing Corporation), the city's Housing Preservation Office, and the Office on Aging's Home Maintenance Repair—received a total of $928,288.[18] Community development block grant funds also supported the repair of some city streets and water lines, the improvement of parks and playgrounds, merchants' efforts to spruce up shopping areas, neighborhood street improvement projects, and storefront renovation.

As the suburb's population declined, council and residents realized that they had to act aggressively to attract new and keep old residents, and like the Cain administration, believed that improving parks was one way to do this. Cain Park's open-air, 3,000-seat theater had been completed in 1938 by the WPA, and in 1944, the city opened a smaller, enclosed theater, the Alma, named after Cain's wife. Under the direction of Dr. Dina Rees Evans, the city produced lavish musical productions in the amphitheater. After Evans retired in 1958, this big stage was used only occasionally for performances of musical artists like Sammy Davis Jr. In 1979, when the amphitheater became the setting for the film *Those Lips, Those Eyes*, the production company restored the sound and lighting systems. When summer outdoor productions resumed in 1980, they were sometimes canceled by inclement weather. In 1987, voters passed a bond issue that allowed the city to install a permanent canopy over the amphitheater. Cain Park contains one of the few municipally owned and operated theaters in the country; its amphitheater was named for Dr. Evans in 1989. The Cain Park Arts Festival, a juried show that attracts exhibitors and buyers from around the country, also contributed to the vitality of Cain Park.

SOMERTON ROAD BLOCK PARTY. This annual event honors patriotism as well as the community's commitment to the arts. (Roy Woda.)

CAIN PARK ARTS FESTIVAL. This annual show attracts exhibitors from all around the United States.(Cleveland Heights Public Relations Department.)

In February 1997, voters approved another bond issue intended primarily for the improvement of parks and recreation facilities. One of those improvements was the renovation of the World War II Memorial in Cumberland Park. A second was a low marble and stone wall built to the west of the first monument to honor the Cleveland Heights men and women who served in the Korean, Vietnam, and Persian Gulf Wars. Twelve Cleveland Heights men died in the Korean War; eleven in the Vietnam War.

No one objected to honoring these servicemen. But most of the $15 million bond issue was for a new community center in Forest Hill Park. This generated another bitter, bruising fight that divided neighbor from neighbor and delayed the building's start for two years. The proposed new structure would much enlarge a recreation pavilion completed in 1969; it would contain two ice rinks, two basketball courts, a senior center, an after-school child-care facility, and meeting rooms. Supporters of the new center included senior citizens, sports enthusiasts, PTA members, and parents of hockey players and figure skaters, who sometimes brought their children to public meetings. Its vocal opponents included historic preservationists who bewailed the center's intrusion into the green space that was the legacy of the Rockefellers; environmentalists who argued that the huge building would damage the park's ecology; and others who simply objected to the building's big, boxy design. Heated debates accompanied every presentation of the proposal to the public and to the Planning Commission, which had jurisdiction over the park. Heated attacks on the proposed building became verbal attacks on the integrity of commission members. In July 1998, the commission, chaired by Robert P. Madison, postponed its decision, and in August, the proposal

NEW WAR MEMORIAL, 2001. Cleveland Heights lost eleven of its young men in the Vietnam war.

did not have enough votes to pass. Jubilant opponents had marshaled support from members of the Rockefeller family, but their victory was short-lived. In January 1999, after the city had appointed three new members, the commission approved an amended proposal in a marathon meeting attended by vocal sign-bearers for both sides. In the meantime, Cleveland Heights had funded a survey of the park by landscape architects Pressley Associates and some initial clean-up efforts. The new community center opened in January 2002, almost five years after the bond issue had passed.

The First Suburbs Consortium represented another attempt to actively address the problems of Cleveland Heights and other members: Bedford, Euclid, Fairview Park, Garfield Heights, Lakewood, Maple Heights, Parma, Shaker Heights, South Euclid, University Heights, and Warrensville Heights. (Two more coalitions of urban suburbs later formed around Cincinnati and Columbus.) Initiated by Cleveland Heights Councilman Kenneth Montlack, the First Suburbs Consortium was a lobbying organization, a political response to the dramatically changed position of older suburbs. These built-up inner-ring suburbs with racially and economically diverse populations had less land to develop than newer communities in Geauga, Medina, and Lake Counties and fewer fiscal resources with which to encourage economic growth. Aided by a grant from the George Gund Foundation, the consortium initiated a low-interest loan program for housing renovation and repair in their communities. Consortium members criticized policy-makers in Columbus and Washington, D.C. for failing to invest in older communities while spending lavishly on highways that hastened the outward migration of residents from Cleveland and its inner-ring suburbs. Planners now called this urban sprawl.

As in the fight against the freeways, the First Suburbs Consortium had the support of environmentalists; multi-lane highways, enormous shopping malls, and new low-density residential developments ate up green space and destroyed farmland. Learning from that earlier victory over County Engineer Albert Porter and the Clark Freeway, the older suburbs recognized the need to join forces and create a united front. And like this earlier battle, the consortium underscored the vital connections between the well-being of the suburbs, the region, and the nation. Cleveland Heights, and other suburbs, had been dramatically altered by recent regional and national developments—the civil rights movement, the decay of inner-city neighborhoods, the decline of heavy industry, and urban sprawl, for instance.

These 30 years had transformed Cleveland Heights in visible ways. Its population was smaller, less white, and sometimes less affluent. Some of its dignified public schools, built in the affluent 1920s, were replaced by smaller, less impressive structures; the suburb's tradition of academic excellence was no longer secure. Houses of worship changed hands and names as former worshippers left the community. The suburb's exclusive shopping center was replaced by a strip mall. Maintenance of private homes required public monies. Aging parks had to be revitalized in order to compete with newer suburbs.

KINGSTON ROAD, JULY 4, 1964. Block parties are an essential tradition in a changing community. (Cleveland Public Library.)

But equally significant, although less tangible, was the redefinition of Cleveland Heights. The "urban suburb" got mixed reviews in the local media. In June 1995, a former resident lamented the suburb's transformation in an article in *Northern Ohio Live* entitled "Nowhere to Run: Problems of a Troubled City": "I used to think Cleveland Heights had all the answers [to racial problems]. Now I am not so sure." On the other hand, Cleveland Heights was also described as "a progressive city," and " a lesson in diversity." According to one local newspaper, "Diverse Cleveland Heights [puts] all that together and [makes] it work." "Diverse eccentricity" characterized the city, said another observer.[19] The city itself used similar terms on its coffee mugs and web page: "vital . . . progressive . . . diverse."

Cleveland Heights had been redefined not by its coffee mugs but by its engaged, active citizens. Beneath official, politically correct rhetoric lay genuine sensitivity to class, race, and religious differences. Black and white, Jewish and non-Jewish, wealthy and not-so-wealthy, citizens had gradually, often painfully, faced the changes that had transformed their community. They became agents of racial equity in housing and education, activists for the preservation of housing and the environment, and advocates of new political strategies and alliances.

At the same time, residents had sustained and renewed important community traditions. Among these were dozens of annual block parties. These had perhaps been initiated by the block groups of World War II, another period when the community pulled together in the face of great changes. Encouraged by the city but organized by residents, block parties provided occasions at which neighbors could greet and meet one another. Often held on the Fourth of July or Labor Day, parties also allowed each street to express its allegiance to the community in its own unique way.

The last controversy of the twentieth century, the battle over the new community center, taught the suburb's leaders about the need for unity at home. Deciding to harness rather than fight the energies of citizens, city council in October 1999 initiated a "visioning" process that would engage residents in imagining a common future for the suburb's second century.

CHATFIELD AND YORKSHIRE ROADS. Block parties are special occasions for children and adults. (Lynn Weygandt and Colleen Olsen.)

EPILOGUE
LOOKING BACKWARD AND FORWARD

The visioning process took almost two years to complete and involved hundreds of citizens attending dozens of meetings. In October 2001, the Visioning Committee presented to city council its final document. Its vision was firmly rooted in the city's past, keenly aware of its present problems, and cautiously optimistic about its future.

The committee found much in Cleveland Heights worth preserving: its beautiful homes and neighborhoods, its parks, green spaces, and pleasant shopping districts. These had attracted people to the suburb for a century. The committee also noted, however, the pressing need to revitalize aging housing and declining commercial areas and to restore the community's confidence in its public schools. Looking to the future, the committee urged that the suburb's tradition of civic activism be maintained and the community's diversity be cherished and nurtured. With understandable hyperbole, the committee summarized: "Cleveland Heights: extraordinary people and extraordinary places."[1]

The 2000 census data described the city in different terms. Since 1990, Cleveland Heights had continued to lose residents as had the cities of Cleveland, Shaker Heights, University Heights, and Lakewood. Far-flung suburbs in Medina, Geauga, and Lake Counties grew rapidly as urban sprawl continued to take its toll. Cleveland Heights's initial population count was below 50,000 for the first time since 1930. A recount demanded by the city's law director found uncounted students in a Case Western Reserve University dormitory, bringing the total to 50,769. At stake were $2 million in community development block grant funds, perhaps lost if the population fell below the 50,000 mark. Even with the adjusted count, the suburb's population had shrunk six percent since 1990. African Americans constituted 42 percent of the 2000 total; they had been joined by a growing number of Asian-American, Hispanic, and multi-racial persons. According to *The Plain Dealer*, Cleveland Heights was the second most racially diverse city in northeast Ohio.[2] The suburb was also economically diverse: home to the very wealthy and to those who lived below the poverty line.

These demographic changes are less startling in historical context. Cleveland Heights, the elite, exclusive suburb, was always something of a myth, a compelling and enormously attractive myth created by real estate developers and fostered by city officials. It had encouraged people of all kinds to move to Cleveland Heights. The farmhouses, apartments, two-family homes, kit houses, modest colonials, and bungalows of its earliest decades testified to the socio-economic diversity of its citizens. So did the residents who worked on city and federal public works projects and the families who received assistance during the Depression. So did the decline and demise of some of the great mansions during and after World War II. So did the rapid, transforming in-migrations of Jews that began in the 1920s and of African Americans, half a century later.

For "the heights" of the suburb had never provided an escape from the city; in fact, the city and the suburb were always intimately connected. The founders of the suburb borrowed Cleveland's name. Patrick Calhoun even borrowed the name of its most famous avenue. To ensure their profits, Calhoun and the Van Sweringens had arranged for streetcars to connect their developments to the city. Despite his resistance to annexation by Cleveland, Frank C. Cain had fought mighty battles to ensure that streetcar service to downtown was good. The streetcar and then the automobile inextricably linked the suburb to the fortunes and misfortunes of the city of Cleveland, its next-door neighbor. Changes in Cleveland's population, the rise and decline of its industrial economy, the

ANNIVERSARY PARADE, 1996. Cleveland Heights marked its 75th anniversary as a city with a colorful parade that celebrated its citizens' energy, enthusiasm, and commitment to their community. (Susie Kaeser and Marian J. Morton.)

146

deterioration of city neighborhoods and race relations, the devastating impact of highways, all had repercussions for the suburb. As the First Suburbs Consortium recognized, the fates of the suburb, the city, the region, and the nation were intertwined.

As Cleveland Heights entered its second century as an independent suburb, residents and leaders faced great challenges. Again, in historical context, these did not appear overwhelming. Residents and leaders of this community had successfully met great challenges before. East Cleveland Township farmers had survived the wilderness, the weather, and the Civil War. Cleveland Heights's first elected officials had created a viable government, retained its political autonomy, and guided the suburb's swift development from a tiny hamlet of 1,500 to a city of 60,000. Citizens had sustained themselves and the community through the catastrophes of the Depression and World War II and had resisted the destruction of the landscape by freeways.

Perhaps the most pressing of the present problems, as the visioning process had acknowledged, was creating and maintaining a shared purpose for an ever-changing, enormously varied community. This was in fact a familiar problem. Even before Cleveland Heights became a city, its northeast corner had attempted to secede. Since then, residents and leaders had adapted, more or less successfully, to the rapid influx of persons of different class, religious, and racial backgrounds. The conflicts and controversies that accompanied these and other changes had not irretrievably torn the fabric of the community.

In 2002, there were no clear signs about the future of Cleveland Heights. Townhouses provided new housing choices in the oldest neighborhoods along Noble Road, Euclid Heights Boulevard, and Fairmount Boulevard. New commercial ventures, often national chains, moved into old sites like Severance Town Center and the Heights Rockefeller Building. City council provided financial incentives, including tax abatements, for new development and for maintaining older homes.

Predicting the future is always difficult. Patrick Calhoun had predicted that Cleveland Heights would always be home to Cleveland's elite; he guessed wrong and lost much of his investment in the community. Mayor Cain had predicted that the city would have a population of 100,000; fortunately, he too guessed wrong.

The Visioning Committee made this prediction: "[C]hanges will be the focused actions of people committed to preserving and maintaining an extraordinary community."[3] This seemed the safest guess. The second safest guess is that the future won't be dull.

147

Bibliography

Books and Articles

Baxandall, Rosalyn, and Elizabeth Ewen. *Picture Windows: How the Suburbs Happened*. New York: Basic Books, 2000.

Bellamy, John Stark. *Angels on the Heights: A History of St. Ann's Parish, Cleveland Heights, Ohio, 1915–1990*. Cleveland: privately printed, 1990.

——. *They Died Crawling and Other Tales of Cleveland Woe*. Cleveland: Gray Publishing, 1995.

Binford, Henry C. *The First Suburbs: Residential Communities on the Boston Periphery, 1815–1860*. Chicago: University of Chicago Press, 1985.

Birkner, Michael J. *A Country Place No More: The Transformation of Bergenfield, New Jersey, 1894–1994*. London and Ontario: Fairleigh Dickinson Press, 1994.

Borchert, James. "From City to Suburb: The Strange Case of Cleveland's Disappearing Elite and Their Changing Residential Landscapes: 1885–1935," *Proceedings of the Ohio Academy of History* (Marion, OH, 2000): 11–30.

——. "Residential City Suburbs: The Emergence of a New Suburban Type, 1890–1930," *Journal of Urban History*, Vol. 22 No. 3 (March 1996): 283-307.

Borchert, Jim and Susan. *Lakewood: The First Hundred Years*. Norfolk, VA.: Donning Company Publishers, 1989.

Caldron. Cleveland: Cleveland Heights High School, 1954.

Caldron. Cleveland: Cleveland Heights High School, 1976.

Caldron. Cleveland: Cleveland Heights High School, 1980.

Cigliano, Jan. *Showplace of America: Cleveland's Euclid Avenue, 1850–1910*. Kent: Kent State University Press, 1991.

Clark, Clifford Edward Jr. *The American Family Home, 1800–1960*. Chapel Hill: University of North Carolina Press, 1986.

The Cleveland Blue Book. Cleveland: Helen DeKay Townsend, 1924.

Cleveland Town Topics, 3 August 1901: 9.

Coates, William R. *History of Cuyahoga County*, Volume 1. Chicago: American Historical Society, 1924.

Contosta, David R. *Suburb in the City: Chestnut Hill, Philadelphia, 1850–1990*. Columbus: Ohio State University Press, 1992.

Ebner, Michael H. *Creating Chicago's North Shore: A Suburban History.* Chicago: University of Chicago Press, 1988.

Fishman, Robert. *Bourgeois Utopias: The Rise and Fall of Suburbia.* New York: Basic Books, 1987.

Gartner, Lloyd P. *History of the Jews of Cleveland.* Cleveland: Western Reserve Historical Society and the Jewish Federation of Cleveland, 1978.

Gordon, Albert I. *Jews in Suburbia.* Boston: Beacon Press, 1959.

Green, H.W. *Census Facts and Trends by Tracts: Special 1954 Report.* Cleveland: Real Property Inventory of Metropolitan Cleveland, 1954.

———. *Jewish Families in Greater Cleveland.* Cleveland: Cleveland Health Council, 1939.

———. *Population Characteristics by Census Tracts—Cleveland, 1930.* Cleveland: *Cleveland Plain Dealer,* 1931.

Groth, Paul, and Todd W. Bressi, editors. *Understanding Ordinary Landscapes.* New Haven and London: Yale University Press, 1997.

Harris, Mary Emma, and Ruth Mills Robinson. *The Proud Heritage of Cleveland Heights, Ohio.* Oberlin: Oberlin Printing Company, 1966.

Hertzberg, Arthur. *The Jews in America: Four Centuries of an Uneasy Encounter.* New York: Simon and Schuster, 1989.

Hughes, Adella Prentiss. *Music Is My Life.* Cleveland: World Publishing, 1947.

Hunker, Henry L. *Columbus, Ohio: A Personal Geography.* Columbus: Ohio State University Press, 2000.

Jackson, Kenneth T. *Crabgrass Frontier: The Suburbanization of the United States.* New York: Oxford University Press, 1985.

Jewish Community Federation of Cleveland. *Survey of Cleveland's Jewish Population, 1987.* Cleveland: Jewish Community Federation, August 1988.

Jewish Community Federation of Cleveland. *1996 Jewish Population Study.* Cleveland: Jewish Community Federation, 1998.

Johnson, Crisfield. *History of Cuyahoga County, Ohio.* Cleveland: Leader Printing Company, 1879; reprint by Whippoorwill Publications, 1984.

Jones, Suzanne Ringler, editor. *In Our Day. Cleveland Heights: Its People, Its Places, Its Past.* Cleveland Heights: Heights Community Congress, 1986.

Keating, W. Dennis. *The Suburban Racial Dilemma: Housing and Neighborhoods.* Philadelphia: Temple University Press, 1994.

Kowinski, William Severini. *The Malling of America: An Inside Look at the Great Consumer Paradise.* New York: Morrow Publishing, 1985.

Kusmer, Kenneth L. *A Ghetto Takes Shape: Black Cleveland, 1870–1930.* Urbana: University of Illinois Press, 1976.

Lake, D.J. *Atlas of Cuyahoga County.* Philadelphia: Titus, Simmons, and Titus, 1874.

Leedy, Walter. "Eric Mendelsohn's Park Synagogue," *Gamut* (Special Issue, 1990): 45–69.

Lipman, Eugene J., and Albert Vorspan, editors. "Cleveland: City Without Jews," in *A Tale of Ten Cities: The Triple Ghetto in American Religious Life.* New York: Union of Hebrew Congregations, 1962.

Logan, John R., and Mark Schneider. "Racial Segregation and Racial Change in

American Suburbs, 1970–1980," *American Journal of Sociology,* Volume 89, Number 4 (1984): 874–888.

Marsh, Margaret. *Suburban Lives.* New Brunswick: Rutgers University Press, 1990.

Meinig. D.W., editor. *The Interpretation of Ordinary Landscapes: Geographical Essays.* New York: Oxford University Press, 1979.

Muller, Peter O. *Contemporary Suburban America.* Englewood Cliffs, NJ: Prentice Hall, 1981.

Munro, Eleanor. *Memoir of a Modernist's Daughter.* New York: Viking Press, 1988.

The Negro in Cleveland, 1950–1963. Cleveland: Cleveland Urban League, 1964.

O'Connor, Carol A. *A Sort of Utopia: Scarsdale, 1891–1981.* Albany: State University of New York, 1983.

Post, Charles Asa. *Doan's Corners and the City Four Miles East.* Cleveland: The Caxton Company, 1930.

Price, Ellen Loughry. *A History of East Cleveland.* East Cleveland: privately published, 1970.

Rose, William Ganson. *Cleveland: The Making of a City.* Cleveland: World Publishing, 1950.

Shulman, Alix Kates. *Memoirs of an Ex-Prom Queen.* Chicago: Cassandra Edition, 1985.

Sinclair, Jo. *The Changelings.* New York: McGraw Hill, 1955.

Sklare, Marshall, and Joseph Greenblum. *Jewish Identity on the Suburban Frontier.* New York: Basic Books, 1967.

Stilgoe, John R. *Borderlands: Origins of the American Suburb, 1820–1939.* New Haven and London: Yale University Press, 1988.

Teaford, John C. *Post-Suburbia: Government and Politics in Edge Cities.* Baltimore: Johns Hopkins University Press, 1997.

Tittle, Diana. *Welcome to Heights High: The Crippling Politics of Restructuring America's Public Schools.* Columbus: The Ohio State University Press, 1995.

Van Tassel, David V., and John Grabowski, editors. *Encyclopedia of Cleveland History.* Bloomington: Indiana University Press, 1987.

Vincent, Sidney Z., and Judah Rubinstein. *Merging Traditions—Jewish Life in Cleveland: A Contemporary Narrative, 1945–1975, A Pictorial Record, 1839–1975.* Cleveland: Western Reserve Historical Society and the Jewish Community Federation of Cleveland, 1978.

Vincent, Sidney Z. *Personal and Professional: Memoirs of a Life in Community Service.* Cleveland: Jewish Community Federation of Cleveland, 1982.

Warner, Sam Bass. *Streetcar Suburbs: The Process of Growth in Boston, 1870–1900.* Cambridge: Harvard University Press and the M.I.T. Press, 1962.

MANUSCRIPTS AND UNPUBLISHED SOURCES

"Annual Report of the Board of Education." Cleveland: East Cleveland Public Schools, 1872.

Barrow, William C. "The Euclid Heights Allotment: A Palimpsest of the Nineteenth-Century Search for Real Estate Value in Cleveland's East End. Master's thesis, Cleveland State University, 1997, *http://www.scuohio.edu/CUT/history/thesis*

B.R. Deming Company. Euclid Golf Allotment. Pamphlet. Western Reserve Historical Society (WRHS), n.d.

Cleveland Heights, Ohio. "Survey of Public School Building Requirements, 1922." Pamphlet. WRHS.

"First Annual Catalogue of the Public Schools of East Cleveland, Ohio." Cleveland: East Cleveland Public Schools, 1806.

Ford Family Papers. MSS 3963. WRHS.

Hamley, Kara. "Cleveland's Park Allotment: Euclid Heights, Cleveland Heights, Ohio and Its Developer, Ernest W. Bowditch." Master's thesis. Cornell University, 1996.

Heights Citizens for Human Rights. MSS 3647, WRHS.

Heylman, Kay and Martin. Deed for Frank C. Cain's home at 1590 Compton Road, *c.* 1921.

Jewish Community Center. MSS 3668, WRHS.

Jewish Community Council of Cleveland. Microfilm Reel 1, WRHS.

Jewish Community Federation of Cleveland. MSS 4563, WRHS.

"The Mayor's Message and Sixth Annual Reports of East Cleveland, Ohio." Cleveland: East Cleveland Village, 1901.

Oakwood Club. MSS 3661, WRHS.

Rubinstein, Judah. "Jewish Suburban Population Movement in Cleveland and Its Impact on Communal Institutions." Cleveland: Jewish Community Federation of Cleveland, 1957.

"Sixth Annual Report of the Superintendent to the Board of Education, Cleveland Heights, 1920–21." Cleveland Heights: Cleveland Heights Board of Education, 1921.

Taylor Family History. MSS 4394, WRHS.

White-Ford Family Papers. MSS 3666, WRHS.

Women's Civic Club of Cleveland Heights. MSS 3641, WRHS.

NEWSPAPERS AND PERIODICALS

Cleveland Plain Dealer
Heights Dispatch
Heights Press
Heights Sun Press
Jewish Independent
Jewish Review and Observer
The Plain Dealer
Sun and Heights Press

PUBLIC RECORDS

Cleveland Heights City Council Minutes. Cleveland Heights City Hall, Cleveland Heights, Ohio.

Cleveland Heights City Manager's Files. LGR MUN 0091, WRHS.

Cleveland Heights City Manager's Journal. LGR-MICR, WRHS.

Cleveland Heights Planning and Zoning Commission Minutes. LGR-MICR, WRHS.

Cuyahoga County Commissioners' Clerk Files. Cuyahoga County Archives, Cleveland, Ohio.

United States Bureau of the Census. Cuyahoga County, Ohio, 1850, 1860, and 1870.

SUPERIOR ROAD SCHOOLHOUSE. Recently renovated, this nineteenth-century schoolhouse is a reminder of the suburb's past as a small rural community; it is on the National Register of Historic Places.

ENDNOTES

CHAPTER 1

1. Chrisfield Johnson. *History of Cuyahoga County, Ohio*, 447.
2. ibid., 444–445.
3. ibid., 77.
4. ibid., 445.
5. Henry Ford to David Ford, August 1, 1845, and Horace Ford to Lewis Ford, November, 1846, MSS 3963, container 1, folder 3, Cyrus Ford Papers, MSS 3963 Western Reserve Historical Society (WRHS), Cleveland, Ohio.
6. Henry Ford to David Ford, August 1, 1845, container l, folder 3, MSS 3963.
7. Horatio C. Ford, Diary, White-Ford Family Papers, MSS 3666, container 5, folder 2, WRHS. "First Annual Catalogue of the Public Schools of East Cleveland, Ohio."
8. United States Bureau of the Census, Cuyahoga County, 1850, 1860, 1870. Population numbers, Johnson, *History of Cuyahoga County*, 210.
9. East Cleveland Public Schools. *Annual Report of the Board of Education*, 25.
10. Johnson. *History of Cuyahoga County*, 447.
11. William Ganson Rose. *Cleveland: The Making of a City*, 500-501.
12. "The Mayor's Message and Sixth Annual Report of East Cleveland, Ohio," 6, 9.
13. ibid., 85, 87, 7.

CHAPTER 2

1. *Cleveland Town Topics*, 3 August 1901: 9; B.R. Deming Company, "Euclid Golf Allotment" (n.d.) Pamphlet, WRHS.
2. United States Bureau of the Census, Cuyahoga County, 1860 and 1870; *First Annual Catalogue of the Public Schools of East Cleveland, Ohio*, 9, 10.
3. Taylor Family History, MSS 4394, WRHS; Personal Recollections (*c.* 1929), Stella Minor Antisdale, Women's Civic Club of Cleveland Heights, MSS 3641, container 3, folder 4, WRHS.
4. John Stark Bellamy II. *They Died Crawling and Other Tales of Cleveland Woe*,

29–46.

5. Suzanne Ringler Jones, editor. *In Our Day. Cleveland Heights: Its People, Its Places, Its Past*, 30-31, 38-39.

6. *Cleveland Plain Dealer*, 16 May 1909: 7-D.

7. B.R. Deming Company, "Euclid Golf Allotment."

8. James Borchert. "From City to Suburb: The Strange Case of Cleveland's Disappearing Elite and Their Changing Residential Landscapes: 1885–1935." *Proceedings of the Ohio Academy of History*, 17.

9. *Cleveland Plain Dealer*, 13 August 1905: D-7; *Cleveland Plain Dealer*, 2 May 1909: D-3.

10. Cleveland Heights, Ohio. "Survey of Public School Building Requirements, 1922," 32, Pamphlet, WRHS.

11. Deed in the possession of Kay and Martin Heylman, owners of Frank C. Cain's home at 1590 Compton Road.

12. Coventry-Mayfield Land Company. Pamphlet 1125, c. 1912. WRHS; *Cleveland Plain Dealer*, 9 May, 1909, 7-D. I am grateful to Deanna Bremer for this information on the Deming developments.

13. H.W. Greene. *Population Characteristics by Census Tracts—Cleveland, 1930.* (Cleveland, 1931), 12, 15.

14. John Stark Bellamy. *Angels on the Heights: A History of St. Ann's Parish, Cleveland Heights, Ohio, 1915–1990* (Cleveland: 1990), 8, 9, 27

15. *Sixth Annual Report of the Superintendent to the Board of Education, Cleveland Heights, 1920–21,* (Cleveland Heights, 1921), 21.

16. Biographies: Frank Clark Cain, MSS 3641, container 1, folder 5, WRHS.

17. City Council Ordinance No. 2337, August 1921, Cleveland Heights City Hall.

CHAPTER 3

1. *Heights Press*, 26 June 1925:1.

2. *Cleveland Heights Dispatch*, 24 June 1926; 2 September 1926: 1.

3. H.W. Greene, quoted in Women's Civic Club of Cleveland Heights, MSS 3641, container 2, folder 2, WRHS; *Cleveland Heights Dispatch*, 4 January 1923: 6.

4. *Heights Press*, 9 April 1926: 1.

5. Judith Cetina, "County Records: A Lens into the Past," Western Reserve Studies Symposium, October 19, 1996.

6. Suzanne Ringler Jones, editor, *In Our Day: Cleveland Heights: Its People, Its Places, Its Past* (Cleveland, 1986), 33–34, 39–40, 52.

7. James Borchert, "Residential City Suburbs: The Emergence of a New Suburban Type, 1890–1930," *Journal of Urban History*, Vol. 22 No. 3 (March 1996); 291–292; James Borchert, "From City to Suburb: The Strange Case of Cleveland's Disappearing Elite and Their Changing Residential Landscape: 1885–1935," *Proceedings of the Ohio Academy of History* (Marion, OH, 1999): 19; *Cleveland Blue Book* (Cleveland, 1924): 259.

8. H.W. Green, *Population Characteristics by Census Tracts*, 1, 54; *Cleveland Heights Dispatch*, 2 August 1923: 1; *Cleveland Plain Dealer*, 5 April 1923: 12-C; *Cleveland Plain Dealer*, 6 May 1928: 16-B.

9. *Cleveland Plain Dealer*, 4 March 1923; 8-C; 1 March 1923: 29; 9 March 1924: 11-B.

10. *Cleveland Plain Dealer*, 2 May 1926: 8-C; 5 May 1929: 7-D; 5 April 1925: 12-C.

11. *Cleveland Heights Dispatch*, 22 October 1925: 4, 5.

12. *Cleveland Heights Dispatch*, 22 November 1923: 2.

13. *Cleveland Plain Dealer*, 18 October 1924: 12.

14. *Cleveland Heights Dispatch*, 17 December 1925: 1.

15. *Cleveland Heights Dispatch*, 24 June 1926: 1; *Heights Press*, 21 June 1929: 1.

16. *Cleveland Heights Dispatch*, 28 August 1924:1; Cleveland Heights City Council Minutes, October 3, 1921.

17. *Heights Press*, 4 July 1924: 1.

18. *Heights Press*, 5 September 1924: 1.

19. "Sixth Annual Report of the Superintendent to the Board of Education, Cleveland Heights, 1920–1921" (Cleveland, Ohio, 1921), 21.

20. H.W. Greene, quoted in Women's Civic Club of Cleveland Heights, MSS 3641, container 1, folder 7, WRHS.

21. *Heights Press*, 17 April 1925: 1.

22. *Heights Press*, 18 April 1939: 1.

CHAPTER 4

1. 18 April 1931, *The Bystander*, quoted in the Women's Civic Club of Cleveland Heights, MSS 3641, container 1, folder 5, WRHS.

2. *Heights Press*, 29 September 1933: 5; 13 October 1933: 1, 3.

3. *Heights Press*, 13 January 1933: 1; 7 July 1933: 3.

4. *Heights Press*, 3 February 1933: 1; 12 May 1933: 1, 2.

5. *Heights Press*, 24 November 1933: 1; 8 December 1933: 2.

6. *Heights Press*, 24 August 1934: 1.

7. *Heights Press*, 12 February 1938: 1.

8. MSS 3641, container 2, folder 2; LGR-MICR, City Manager's Journal, January 29, 1935 and August 31, 1935, Roll 001, WRHS.

9. *Heights Press*, 7 July 1939: 3.

10. *Heights Press*, 6 October 1939: 1; 17 November 1939: 2.

11. Suzanne Ringler Jones, editor. *In Our Day: Cleveland Heights, Its People, Its Places, Its Past* (Cleveland, 1986), 47.

12. Jones, *In Our Day*, 52, 59, 62, 43, 54.

13. *Heights Press*, 20 September 1940: 1.

14. *Heights Press*, 21 March 1941: 1; 18 July 1941: 1.

15. *Heights Press*, 23 January 1942: 1; 30 January 1942: 1; 2 October 1942: 1.

16. *Heights Press*, 10 April 1942: 1; 31 July 1942: 1.

17. *Heights Press*, 24 July 1942: 4.
18. *Heights Press*, 25 February 1942, 1; 15 March 1942: 1.
19. *Heights Press*, 29 June 1944: 5.
20. Alix Kates Shulman. *Memoirs of an Ex-Prom Queen*, 23.
21. *Heights Press*, 21 December 1944: 4; 23 August 1945: 3.
22. *Cleveland Plain Dealer*, 25 March 1934: A-22; *Heights Press*, 3 February 1944: 1; 4 January 1945: 1; 20 July 44: 2.
23. *Heights Press*, 8 November 1945: 3; 29 November 1945: 11; 24 November 1945: 4.
24. *Heights Press*, 10 January 1946: 9.

Chapter 5

1. Eleanor Munro. *Memoir of a Modernist's Daughter*, 35, 91–92.
2. H.W. Green. *Census Facts and Trends by Tracts: Special 1954 Report*, 28, 30.
3. *Sun Press,* 11 June 1959: 1; 17 June 1965: 1.
4. *Sun Press*, 18 June 1953: 31.
5. Vertical file, "Severance Center," Cleveland Heights, OH, WRHS.
6. Regional Planning Commission, Annual Report, 1954, 25, City Manager's Files, LGR-MUN 0091, container 45, folder "Regional Planning - Mayfield Taylor Area," WRHS.
7. *Heights and Sun Press*, 20 May 1954: 17; 12 August 1954: 13.
8. *Heights and Sun Press*, 8 September 1949: 1.
9. *Heights Sun Press*, 12 December 1963: B-10.
10. *Heights Sun Press*, 9 January 1964: A-1; 14 January 1965: A-2; 5 March 1964: A-1; 5 August 1965: A-1.
11. *Heights Sun Press*, 22 January 1970: A-2.
12. *Heights and Sun Press*, 1 October 1953: 1.
13. *Heights Sun Press*, 2 January 1964: 1; 6 February 1964: 1; 30 April 1964: 1; 5 February 1970: A-10.

Chapter 6

1. B'nai Jeshurun, MSS 4726, scrapbook, container 5, WRHS.
2. Sidney Z. Vincent and Judah Rubinstein. *Merging Traditions - Jewish Life in Cleveland. A Contemporary Narrative 1945–1975. A Pictorial Record 1839–1975*, 3.
3. Lloyd Gartner. *History of the Jews in Cleveland*, 268.
4. *Jewish Review and Observer*, 9 July 1920: 8; 12 March 1920: 6.
5. Gartner, Lloyd. *History of the Jews*, 271.
6. *Heights Press*, 28 January 1927, Quoted in Women's Civic Club of Cleveland Heights, MSS 3641, container l, folder 7, WRHS.
7. Jones. *In Our Day. Cleveland Heights: Its People, Its Places, Its Past*, 44.
8. B'Nai Jeshurun, MSS 4726, scrapbook, container 5, WRHS.
9. *Cleveland Heights Dispatch*, 24 June 1924: 1.

10. Green. *Population Characteristics by Census Tracts – Cleveland, 1930*, 14.

11. Jones. *In Our Day. Cleveland Heights: Its People, Its Places, Its Past*, 52, 59, 62.

12. Green. *Jewish Families in Greater Cleveland*, 6, Map 3.

13. Rubinstein. *Jewish Suburban Population Movement in Cleveland and Its Impact on Communal Institutions*, 3.

14. *Heights Press*, 3 July 1945: 1.

15. *Heights Press*, 19 June 1947: 1.

16. *Cleveland Heights Caldron* (1939), 114, 134, 131.

17. *Sun and Heights Press*, 15 April 1950: 1; 31 May 1951: 1; *Cleveland Heights Caldron* (1954), 140; Diana Tittle. *Welcome to Heights High: The Crippling Politics of Restructuring America's Public Schools*, 2; *Sun Press*, 7 October 1965: A-3; 7 May 1970: B-3.

18. Jo Sinclair. *The Changelings*, 31, 41.

CHAPTER 7

1. *The Negro in Cleveland, 1950–1963*, 25.

2. W. Dennis Keating. *The Suburban Racial Dilemma: Housing and Neighborhoods*, 77–95.

3. H.W. Green. *Population Characteristics by Census Tracts - Cleveland, 1930*, 14; John J. Grabowski and Diane Ewart Grabowski. *Cleveland: A History in Motion*, 146; H.W. Green. *Census Facts and Trends*, 28; Keating. *The Suburban Racial Dilemma*, 135.

4. *Sun Press*, 18 June 1964; 30 July 1964; 21 October 1965: 1; 7 July 1966: 1; 18 May 1967: 1; 2 September 1976: A-4; 20 February 1968: 1; 21 September 1972: 1.

5. Keating, W. Dennis. *Suburban Racial Dilemma*, 116.

6. *Sun Press*, 13 April 1972: A-1, A-6.

7. "A Statement of Policy by Cleveland Heights City Council," 21 November 1966, Heights Citizens for Human Rights, MSS 3647, container 2, folder 5, WRHS.

8. *Sun Press*, 2 October 1969: A-14; 30 October 1969: A-12.

9. *Sun Press*, 8 November 1973: 1; Keating. *Suburban Racial Dilemma*, 124.

10. Cleveland Heights City Council, Minutes 15 March 1976, Cleveland Heights University Heights Main Library.

11. Cleveland Heights City Council, Resolutions 26-1976, 27-1976, and 26-1976 amended, November 19, 1979.

12. Keating. *Suburban Racial Dilemma*, 63.

13. Jewish Community Federation. *Survey of Cleveland's Jewish Population, 1987*, 17, 18; Jewish Community Federation. *1996 Jewish Population Study*, 16, 42; Lauren B. Raffe, director of research, Jewish Community Federation, e-mail to the author, 20 March 2002.

14. *Plain Dealer*, 20 June 1991: 8-A; *Sun Press*, 18 January 2001: A-3.

15. *Sun Press*, 15 March 1973: B-3.

16. 2000–2001 Annual Report of Cleveland Heights–University Heights Board of Education. *School Days* (Winter 2002): unpaged.
17. *Plain Dealer*, 13 January 2002: H-1, H-3; 2000–2001 Annual Report of Cleveland Heights–University Heights Board of Education.
18. *2001 Community Development Block Grant, Consolidated Annual Performance and Evaluation Report. Grant Number B-01-MC-005*, 6.
19. "Nowhere to Run (Problems of a Troubled City)," *Northern Ohio Live*: 68; "Cleveland Heights: A Progressive City," *Cleveland Magazine,* 1 November 1990, 65; "Only in Cleveland Heights," *Northern Ohio Live,* (June 1993): Special Section, 33; *Plain Dealer*, 20 January 1985, A-25; *Sun Press*, 2 November: A-1.

EPILOGUE

1. "Cleveland Heights Visioning Summary," November 2001, 3-8.
2. *Plain Dealer*, 17 March 2001: 8-A; *Sun Press*, 31 May 2001: A-8; *Sun Press*, 30 August 2001: A-7; *Plain Dealer*, 18 March 2001: 6-A.
3. "Cleveland Heights Visioning Summary," 11.

THE FACES OF THE PRESENT. *These children represent the diversity of present-day Cleveland Heights. (Reaching Heights.)*

INDEX